CHARTED DESIGNS FOR NEEDLE-MADE RUGS

BY SIBYL I. MATHEWS

DOVER PUBLICATIONS, INC., NEW YORK

Published in Canada by General Publishing Com-
pany, Ltd., 30 Lesmill Road, Don Mills, Toronto,
Ontario.
Published in the United Kingdom by Constable
and Company, Ltd., 10 Orange Street, London
WC 2.

This Dover edition, first published in 1976, is an
unabridged and unaltered republication of the work
first published in 1968 in London by Mills & Boon,
Ltd. This edition is published by special arrange-
ment with the original American publisher, Hearth-
side Press, Inc., 445 Northern Blvd., Great Neck,
New York 11021.

International Standard Book Number: 0-486-23264-6
Library of Congress Catalog Card Number: 75-21350

Manufactured in the United States of America
Dover Publications, Inc.
180 Varick Street
New York, N.Y. 10014

Contents

Acknowledgements

Warm thanks are due to those who have helped in the production of this book:
Mr N. P. Birley, Mrs Chisholm, Bishop and Mrs Cockin, Mrs Gibson,
Mrs Gladwin, Mrs Mileham, Miss Ord, Mrs Russell, Miss Alison M.
Smith and Mr H. E. Turner for designing or lending charts.

Mrs Joan Droop, who kindly supplied the instructions for the needle-made adaptation of Rya rugs.

The Embroiderers' Guild for permission to reproduce two transfers.

The National Federation of Women's Institutes for permission to use some matter from a booklet written for them by S.I.M.

The Victoria and Albert Museum for permission to use some matter from their publication *Finnish Rugs* (1958).

Mr J. D. Macqueen and Messrs Robert Hale Ltd, for permission to adapt line-drawings from Mr Macqueen's book *Babylon*.

Above all, I wish to acknowledge my immense debt to my husband, without whose constant encouragement and help this book could never have materialised.

S.I.M.

For
ROSALIND ORD and MARY RUSSELL
who have given such
invaluable help in the production
of this book
and for
All those pupils whom it has been
my privilege and pleasure
to teach and who, in their turn,
have taught me so much

Introduction

The fulfilment of a hope brings great happiness, and it has been a most heartening experience to learn how *Needle-made Rugs* has helped both beginners and knowledgeable rug makers in the production of their own individual designs as well as in the technical aspects of rug making.

One of the major objects of that book (apart from the obviously necessary technical instructions) was to do just this, i.e. to help people to work out and/or adapt their own patterns and ideas, and therefore full-scale rug designs were deliberately excluded. However, the continuing requests for help as regards design have latterly made it seem somewhat churlish to leave unused, rough and unfinished but obviously possible rug designs lying idle in a drawer.

Moreover, increasing years have brought to my husband and myself the realisation that we ourselves could never make half the rugs envisaged. We therefore decided to offer rug makers a collection of fully worked out designs in the hope that they would give pleasure and prove to be useful.

At its inception this seemed a comparatively simple scheme, but very soon we realised that charting a rug occasionally for our own amusement, even if of an elaborate design, was a very different matter from charting enough designs for a worth-while book, and the publisher's dictum of 'at least forty charts, please' seemed a far-away dream.

Then came two turning-points: first a morning spent at the Fitzwilliam Museum at Cambridge with an artist friend who remarked, 'I should like to try to adapt forms from some of those superb rugs for your book'; and then a visit to Florence with another artist friend who promptly became a rug-making enthusiast when faced with the excitement of a large picture by Fra Angelico in which a peculiarly fascinating rug happened to be depicted and which cried out to be reproduced as a real rug.

It is this collaboration of friends and of several rug-making pupils who have sent designs, that has not only enabled the project to be completed but has enlarged the scope of the original plan, and we are most grateful for their unstinted help.

On page 73 of *Needle-made Rugs* mention was made of sources of design for rugs and suggestions given of how and where to look for these and so produce individual results while avoiding the obsession of that over-worked word 'original'. The further the study of rugs is taken, the more certain becomes the truism that 'there is nothing new under the sun' and as the work on this book has developed this has become more and more obvious and has suggested fascinating side-lines to follow up.

For instance, when spending a day in the Library of the Victoria and Albert Museum it was intriguing to come across the design of an old Rya rug in which the very simple field pattern had a distinct family resemblance to that of the Roman mosaic pavement discovered a few years ago when the great Autostrada between Rome and Naples was being made.

An inherited Bokhara rug (which, incidentally, yielded many patterns that were most useful for the amateur rug maker) included among its attractive motifs that of the little stylised, pointed 'trees' which appear so frequently on such rugs, and interest was added to the rug when we saw a photograph of the above Roman pavement with the trees making its border.

These are but two instances; endless such sources can be discovered and the charm of pattern hunting cannot be over-emphasised. It was only when the charts for this book had been gathered together that it was realised that the world had been encircled—from England via France, Italy, Greece, Turkey, Persia, China, Fiji, the U.S.A. and so back to England.

It is the hope of those who have contributed to this book that the readers who find pleasure in working rugs from the charts will perhaps gain added enjoyment from starting to make their own designs.

The wish to create something completely worth while—be it that of a child intent upon building the perfect sand-castle at the sea-side, or Sir Christopher Wren meditating on St Paul's—is deeply imbued in the majority of people, and the result of this desire can be one of the most satisfying of experiences.

Explanatory Notes

As this is specifically a book of rug charts, the emphasis being on design, detailed instructions regarding rug-making in general do not fall within its scope. Many readers will already have knowledge of rug-making technique, and for those Mary Thomas's *Dictionary of Embroidery Stitches,* which gives numerous useful and concise stitch instructions, may supply such extra information as they require. For those, however, who have no idea how to make a beginning, I am bound to suggest, with all diffidence, that they obtain my earlier book, *Needle-made Rugs,* in order to acquire this necessary knowledge. Both these books can be borrowed from a public library.

To deal adequately with a beginner's needs from the start to finish of a rug in this second book would entail repeating all the detailed information in the first.

A few technical points have, however, come to light during the last few years and these will be found in the following notes or in those which accompany each chart.

MATERIALS — CANVAS, WOOL AND NEEDLES

Canvas Foundation
According to the number of double bars per inch, canvas will be specified as being 5s, 7s, etc.

For use with most of these charts standard sizes of good quality open mesh canvas are recommended, having a strong cotton foundation for coarse rugs (3s, 4s and 5s) and a linen one for fine rugs (7s upwards). At the time of writing (spring 1967) the only 7s canvas available is a very good quality foreign make 36 inches wide with 237 double bars in the width. There is a 7s canvas in cotton on the market in various widths but unfortunately it becomes rather soft in the working and is liable to pull out of shape. Since the making of a fine rug takes a considerable time it is strongly recommended that the linen canvas be used even if the wish for a rug narrower than 36 inches entails the sacrifice of some of the canvas – which can always be used for a stitch sampler.

In order to ensure clarity, individual notes are appended to each design, mentioning size of mesh, width of canvas, length of finished rug according to the chart (it being possible in many cases to lengthen this if so desired), approximate weight of wool required and any particular points of interest regarding the design.

A large number of the charts are designed for open mesh 5s canvas, 27 inches wide, this being not so large a canvas as to daunt a beginner and yet of a size to fulfil its function as a floor-covering and to offer possibilities of an interesting design. Larger designs follow on 36-inch-wide canvas, also 5s, and then some more elaborate patterns in varying widths using fine 7s.

Unfortunately, owing to the page size of this book it has been found impracticable to chart any designs for 10s canvas. All the charts have had to be reduced greatly in size from the originals as drawn and it has been found that 36-inch-wide 7s canvas is the largest size that can be used consistent with clarity. It is hoped, however, that enthusiasts, especially when they have made rugs on 7s canvas, will feel capable of designing with enjoyment their own fine rugs on 10s.

Rugs have also been charted to be worked on two different single mesh foundations:

1. An evenly woven, pliable jute, pleasant to handle, with a count of 8 threads to the inch which equals 4 bars of open mesh.

2. A single mesh open canvas which has 10 holes to the inch is admirable when combinations of stitches entailing the use of tent-stitch are used. This is often the case with church work, particularly for communion-rail kneelers, the lengths of which entail an enormous amount of work. Religious symbols and other decoration can often be worked in fine stitches and a great deal of time saved by the use of a bolder stitch for the background.

As an example, if fine tent-stitch (worked over a single intersection, i.e. over one warp and one weft) is used for the detailed motifs, cross-stitch, which equals in size 4 such tent-stitches, or long-legged cross-stitch, could be used for the background.

This latter canvas is available in both linen and cotton mesh (see Appendix 2).

Certain other special matters relating to canvas need mention:

1. When sending quotations for canvas, the suppliers always refer to the number of holes per inch. It should be remembered, however, that with needle-made rugs each stitch is worked over the intersection of warp and weft double bars, represented by one square on the chart. Thus, when designing for these rugs it is the double bars which are counted and not the holes, and there is one less double bar in the width of the canvas than there are holes.

2. An extremely useful point to master is that of 'losing' or 'gaining' a stitch in the canvas width, which is referred to in the notes accompanying certain of the charts. It will be found that it is often easier to design a satisfactory rug with a centre *stitch* in the width rather than a centre *line* between stitches. One of the reasons for this is that the odd stitch gives the possibility of having a motif with a point in the centre of the width of the rug.

If the size of the canvas selected has an even number of double bars (e.g. 27-inch 5s canvas with 134 double bars) it can be converted into an odd number of stitches either by 'losing' a stitch, i.e. working the edging-stitch over the last double bar as well as over the selvedge, or 'gaining' a stitch by utilising two threads of the selvedge as the extra double bar (stitch).

The best way of finishing the edge of a rug is to fold back the selvedge and then work the edging-stitch over the folded selvedge (see *Needle-made Rugs,* page 32).

When a stitch is 'lost' this will mean that the turned-back selvedge will be wider than usual, and to equalise matters the opposite selvedge should *not* be doubled back.

When a stitch is 'gained' by using two threads from the selvedge this selvedge edge should not be turned back as it will already be about the same width as the opposite selvedge which *has* been turned back.

If it is desired to work a design in Soumak, one of the most fascinating of rug stitches, which requires one more double bar in the width of the canvas than the number of stitches shown on the chart, that additional double bar can be taken out of the selvedge in the same way. Using this procedure many of the designs for smooth-faced rugs can be worked in Soumak stitch.

3. Readers may come across other makes of canvas in which the count is not necessarily the same as the standard ones already mentioned. If this difference arises the 'losing' or 'gaining' may prove useful.

4. It may happen that a rug of a special size is required for which all the standard widths of canvas are unsuitable. In such cases it is necessary to cut the nearest standard canvas to the required width, bind the cut edge and work the edging-stitch over the binding. Further details of this method will be found in the notes accompanying Chart 32.

5. When working from a rug chart particular attention should be given to the number of stitches in the border stripes, since when designing these it is frequently necessary to make slight adjustments in order that the motifs in the four corners may be symmetrical. This can be done by lengthening or shortening one or more of the motifs by 1 or 2 stitches which will not be noticeable in the finished rug (see *Needle-made Rugs,* the Design Chart, page 91). It is usually most satisfactory to make this adjustment at each end of the border stripes, although sometimes it is more convenient for it to be at the centre of each end and/or side of the rug. An examination of several of the charts in this book (e.g. Charts 26 and 31) will make this point clear.

6. For clarity when working, the centre stitch (or centre line as the case may be) on the width and length of the charts is marked with two dots for the former and one dot for the latter.

The following table is given as a guide for the correct thicknesses of wool to use with the various canvases:

Double Mesh Canvas	Suitable amount of wool to use in the needle
4s	Used specially for 'Rya' rugs, 4 lengths of 2-ply thrums
5s	Two or sometimes 1 length of 2-ply thrums (depending on the thickness of the wool) or enough lengths of Brussels thrums to cover the canvas
7s	One length of thrums or an adequate number of lengths of Brussels thrums

Single Mesh Canvas

Eight threads to the inch jute, equals 4 bars of double mesh canvas	Two lengths of 2-ply thrums
Single mesh 10s 'open' canvas	As for 7s above

Wool

The types of wool recommended for the rugs charted are those mentioned in the above table, i.e. 2-ply thrums and Brussels thrums (known also as worsted). If the latter is difficult to get, crewel wool can be used, but its texture is really too soft for floor-coverings and also, for a rug, its price is exorbitant. Sometimes a solution of the problem is to use what Brussels thrums can be obtained and then make up with crewel wool, especially as the colour range is likely to be larger than that of the Brussels thrums.

A good quality of wool can be relied on from any of the suppliers listed in Appendix 2, but prices vary and the importance of asking for prices and samples from several firms cannot be emphasised too strongly.

However good the overall quality of the thrums may be, there are sometimes slight variations in its thickness.

When working the Noah's Ark Rug (Chart 38), it was found that the blue thrums for the background was too thick for two lengths to be used but too thin for only one length. Therefore, during the working, one length was 'laid' across the centre of the stitches throughout the width and long-legged cross-stitch worked across the laid threads with most satisfactory results.

A problem to be faced by individual rug makers is the quantity of wool that will be needed for a given sized rug. It is difficult and often impossible to estimate this with a close degree of accuracy owing to the number of factors involved, including the human one, i.e. a beginner is likely to use more wool than an experienced worker.

An intricate pattern will almost certainly involve the use of many colours and different shades of the same colour, and the resulting continual stopping and starting is bound to entail an appreciable amount of waste.

However, it is seldom that the surplus cannot be worked into a later rug, once a rug maker always a rug maker, and unwanted 'left-overs' can be home-dyed a dark colour that will be invaluable for outlines and dividers. The table below is appended as a rough guide for quantities. It is based on the average weight of wool in a number of rugs worked in various stitches and of many sizes, and over the years has been found to be reliable. Waste and variations of stitch have been allowed for by an ample margin of error so that the figures should be on the high side, especially for Soumak, of all stitches the most economical in wool.

Canvas	Type of Stitch	Approximate number of ounces of wool per square foot
4s	Short pile using thrums	8 oz.
4s	Smooth-faced (flat-stitch) using thrums	7 oz.
5s	Short pile or smooth-faced using thrums	6 oz.
7s to 10s	Either short pile or smooth-faced, 2-ply or Brussels thrums according to the canvas	5½ oz.

In the notes accompanying each chart the estimated total amount of wool required is given.

Needles

Needles should be blunt-pointed and sufficiently large for the wool to slip easily through the eye. Sizes 13 to 16 are advised for coarse canvas and 16 to 22 for 7s upwards.

STITCHES

Throughout the notes the suggestions on these are intended for guidance and not as hard and fast rules.

When studying the individual chart notes it will be seen that the stitches for the various rugs fall into two categories – pile and smooth-faced.

With pile rugs it is advisable, and adds to the wearing qualities of the rug, that one row of long-legged cross-stitch should be worked between the edging-stitch and the pile throughout the rug.

For smooth-faced rugs many of the canvas work stitches can be used, but it should be noted that although all rug stitches are suitable for canvas work (with the exception of the very long pile), all canvas work stitches are by no means desirable for rugs.

Strength to withstand the hardest wear is essential, the canvas must be well and truly covered, and diagonal stitches, especially those that cross each other, are recommended.

It will be noticed in the chart notes that a combination of cross-stitch and long-legged cross-stitch is frequently suggested. Both stitches are easy and pleasant to work (the rhythm of the backwards and forwards directions of the long-legged is delightful and soothing), they are economical in wool, lend themselves to shading and wear excellently. A large rug, 6 feet 6 inches by 10 feet 6 inches, worked entirely in these two stitches, has had the hardest possible wear for four years without a sign of deterioration.

It should be noted here that as a single cross-stitch is not so thick as long-legged cross-stitch, it is recommended that it should be reinforced by doubling the lower half of the stitch, which will add to its strength and wearing qualities and also produce the same texture for both stitches.

All the stitches required, with the exception of double-cross rice stitch, are illustrated and described in *Needle-made Rugs,* and many of them can be found in other reference books easily available to the rug maker. Only two will therefore be shown here: Double-Cross Rice Stitch and Soumak Stitch. The latter is included because, owing to its comparatively late introduction, it does not appear in such well-established works as Mary Thomas's *Dictionary of Embroidery Stitches.* As it is one of the most fascinating of all stitches recommended for smooth-faced rugs, it would be a pity if readers could not have the opportunity of trying it.

Double-Cross Rice Stitch

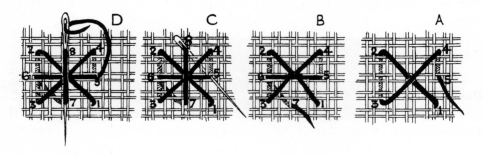

Completion of the stitch from D. The needle having come out at 7 it goes:

In at 5 and out at 6,

In at 8 and out at 7,

In at 6 and out at 3, where it is ready to start the next large cross.

This is a very quick and entertaining stitch to work and it is at times pleasurable to cover the ground rapidly. It is, however, rather a 'luxury' stitch as it will be seen that it stands out somewhat above the other stitches and therefore is inclined to take the first signs of wear. For this reason it is best to use it chiefly in rows where if necessary it can be unpicked and reworked with ease – although that will not be until the rug has had many years of overall hard wear.

Soumak Stitch

Soumak is a stitch that should be used by itself. It is a little intricate to master, but the effort is well worth while. Apart from the actual working being particularly fascinating, it has endless shading possibilities.

This stitch belongs to the interlocking group, and rugs made by this method seem to wear indefinitely. Probably the reason for this is largely that, apart from close interlocking, the surface of rugs made in this way is particularly smooth with correspondingly even distribution of friction.

When worked, this stitch is similar in appearance to stocking-stitch in knitting, and there is a version of it that is actually called Knitting-Stitch. This, however, takes two rows to produce the surface effect that Soumak stitch does in one row, and moreover does not interlock. A special feature of Soumak stitch is that each completed stitch finishes at the hole where it started, thus enabling the worker to travel easily in several directions and so work patterns in the most convenient way. It is often a great help, especially when working a fine rug, to be able to put in the outline of an elaborate motif first and then fill it in, and this is especially simple to do when using Soumak stitch.

When working this stitch the canvas should be held at right-angles to the position used for most rug stitches, i.e. with the unworked canvas to the left of the worker and the selvedges running sideways across the knees. In whichever direction the stitches travel, the V which each stitch makes should have its sharp point facing towards the worker. The resemblance to Soumak weaving is lost if the stitch is incorrectly worked so that the V made by each stitch points along the warp of the canvas instead of along the weft as it should do.

Method of Working

1. Each stitch is begun between the two threads of a canvas weft double bar (i.e. splitting the bar) at hole 1. The needle is then taken up *over* two warp double bars into hole 2, *under* a weft double bar of two threads from right to left into hole 3, returns to the original starting-point at hole 1 and, if a straight line downwards is required, drops down between the threads of the next weft double bar to hole 4. The stitch is then repeated exactly as before. The diagrams marked A show this process in complete detail. The selvedge edge is understood to be at the top of the diagram in each case.

2. Should the worker wish to proceed in a straight line from right to left, the needle is

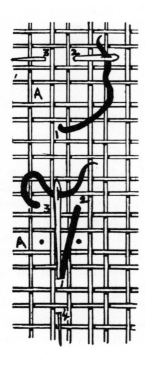

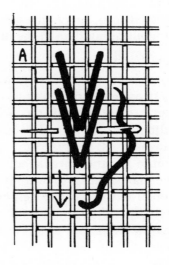

18

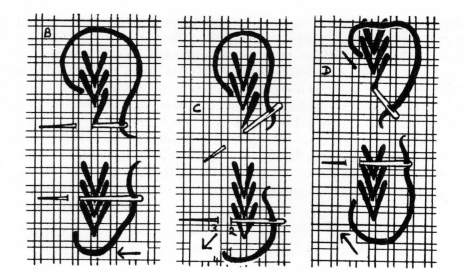

inserted between the double weft bar to the *left* of the finished stitch instead of dropping down, see diagram B.

3. For a diagonal line downwards from right to left, the needle drops *down* one bar diagonally each time, see diagram C.

4. For a diagonal line upwards from right to left, the needle moves *up* one bar diagonally, see diagram D.

In all four cases it must be remembered that *each single stitch in turn* must be worked and completed according to the directions for 1 (above), i.e. from hole 1, via 2 and 3 and back to 1, continuing then in the direction required as shown in the diagrams.

Pitfalls and Hints

1. The stitch is incredibly easy to work when once the basic method has been mastered, but some people find difficulty in remembering that it is always the *weft* double bars (which run straight towards the worker when the canvas is held in the correct position for this stitch) that are split. The fact that there are two threads in each warp double bar in the canvas must be forgotten when working the stitch, and if workers find any temptation to put their needle between these the remedy is to bind them together with thread and make them into one until the working of the stitch becomes mechanical. It is this continual splitting of the weft bars that makes it far easier to use double rather than single mesh canvas for Soumak stitch. The count of the stitch can be very irritating with single mesh wherein two successive equidistant threads have to be treated as a single weft or warp double bar.

2. *Direction:* It is, of course, possible to work straight upwards; from left to right in straight lines; diagonally down from left to right; diagonally up from left to right; in fact in the four opposite directions to those suggested and shown on the diagrams. The reason for not recommending these directions is that the action for their working is clumsy, being somewhat back-handed, but it is sometimes useful to work in these

ways even if awkward. It is however advisable to become thoroughly proficient first with the four easier methods of travelling. On the other hand for a left-handed worker these would be the most natural directions to use.

3. *Outlines and Filling In:* It is a good plan to experiment with the outlines of a small pattern and its filling in before embarking upon a complete rug so as to see how the stitches fit in with each other. When filling in it is easy to omit occasional stitches if care is not exercised.

4. *Designing for a Soumak rug:* It must be remembered always that each stitch is worked over two warp bars of the canvas, so that in designing a rug on squared paper for Soumak stitch the number of squares used in the width must be one less than the number of double bars between the selvedges of the canvas, e.g. if the canvas has 135 double bars in its width there must be only 134 squares (i.e. stitches) shown on the paper.

5. *Importance of Accuracy:* It is not easy to rectify mistakes when making Soumak rugs as the stitches are so closely interlocked that unpicking is difficult; therefore complete accuracy in working is essential. As mentioned before, it is partly this interlocking that ensures the long-wearing qualities of these rugs, while at the same time they are economical in wool and correspondingly light in weight.

6. *Back-Stitch Finish:* Where the stitch meets the selvedges it is necessary to work a row of back-stitches between the Vs and the edging-stitch when the rug is finished, otherwise a gap is left which shows the canvas and spoils the final appearance of the rug.

7. *Working through the 'double' canvas* at the cut ends is particularly tiresome in this stitch, and when very fine canvas is used doubling over can be avoided by machining several times along the last two or three rows of the canvas, then machining a length of narrow binding over this rough edge and finally working the edging-stitch over this. When this method of finishing the edges is adopted the corners may show a slight tendency to curl, in which case it is advisable to attach rubber angle pieces at each corner. These can be obtained in varying sizes from good furnishers. An alternative plan is to work long-legged cross-stitch over an inch of the 'double' at the end of the rug and then to start on the Soumak stitch. This results in a firmer edge but does not look so well.

8. *Tension of Stitch:* Finally, of all stitches Soumak needs most care as regards the tension applied to the wool. This should never be more than the minimum necessary to pull the wool through the canvas, and the thickness of the wool in the needle should not exceed what allows it to pass easily between the split weft bars.

For this reason, and bearing in mind that thrums wool sometimes varies in thickness – two lengths of 2-ply *can* be too thick for Soumak on 5s, and one is sometimes not enough – it is a good idea to work Soumak stitch in Brussels thrums in what is found to be the requisite number of lengths, or one length of 2-ply thrums with one strand of Brussels or crewel wool of a near shade.

COLOUR

Had all the charts in this book been coloured its cost, of course, would have been astronomical – hence the written colour suggestions for each chart and the use of shading to indicate important colour changes. On the whole the simpler charts have been given fuller notes than the more elaborate ones, it being felt that the experienced rug makers would be able, and would prefer, to act on their own initiative.

Several of the books mentioned in the Bibliography are helpful regarding this immense subject of colour (note particularly the beautiful coloured illustrations in Hermann Haack's book), and the study of Oriental rugs will supply endless ideas.

A few special points are here mentioned to co-ordinate with the individual chart notes:
1. The dividers: These are the long, straight lines that make the framework of the border (or borders), the divisions between the border stripes and those between the patterns in a striped rug.

Browns are generally advised for the dividers, it having been found from experience that different shades of brown show up other colours well but do not obtrude themselves too much on the pattern. This, and other colour advice or suggestions, is not arbitrary as the whole matter is so much one of personal taste.
2. If two dividers, each 2 stitches wide, enclose a border stripe, an attractive effect can be produced if two shades of the same colour are used for each, the same shade being on the sides touching the border stripe.
3. The edging-stitch should normally be worked in the same colour as that chosen for the first row of the border, which will be the first row of the framework of the rug. Rugs with end borders only (see Charts 8, 9, 19 and 32), should, of course, have an edging-stitch worked throughout their length as well as their width.
4. Various shades of brown are also often used for the outlining of motifs, but these outlines can be equally effective when worked in either a different shade of the motif or a different colour altogether, i.e. a light red motif can have a dark red outline or vice versa, a yellow motif a blue or green outline, etc. Obviously the colour of the motifs themselves, and therefore their outlines, will be partly governed by the colour of their background.

It is better to use a dark colour for the motifs if the general background is light and again vice versa.
5. The predominating colour of a rug is bound to be the one selected for the 'field' (i.e. the inside of the border framework), and about two-thirds of the field can be worked in this colour, preferably combined with several of its near shades.
6. It helps to co-ordinate the whole colour scheme and design if some of this predominating colour is introduced into the border, care being taken to ensure that the general tone of the border is darker than the field. If the border tone is lighter than that of the field, the picture is inclined to look as if it is liable to drop out of the frame.
7. Careful consideration should be given to the proposed position of the finished rug, i.e. a dark corner needs a bright rug. A wise plan before starting work is to cast a bundle of wool, of the shades being considered, on to the floor where the rug is to lie and to study the effect for several days before coming to a final decision as to the main colour scheme.

Making a rug is a long-term occupation. A worth-while rug cannot be worked in a few hours and therefore it is wise to spend some of that most valuable of all commodities, 'time', in order to consider the project carefully and so to achieve a supremely satisfying result.

CHART 1   The Dolphin Rug

JUTE   4s (See Materials, Note 1, page 12)
WIDTH   36", 144 stitches
LENGTH   62½", 250 stitches
Area of rug: 15¾ sq. ft.
Approximate weight of wool required: 8 lbs.

The dolphins are the outstanding feature of this rug although they appear only in the border. Seaweed forms the outside, narrow border, while the sea fills the field.

Stitches recommended

Surrey stitch or Turkey knot short pile.

Colour suggestions

1. Edging-stitch and two dark dividers – wine.
2. The three single dividers – pale blue.
3. The two stitch dividers each side of the Dolphin border – mid-green.
4. The narrow seaweed border – dark brown with a mid-green background.
5. Dolphin border background – shades of cream.
6. Dolphins – two shades of wine with light blue spots if desired.
7. The field should be in various shades of sea blues and greens, with some of the narrow sections in cream for the tops of the waves.

Design and colour suggestions by Miss Rosalind Ord, Marlborough.

CHART 1

The Dolphin Rug

CHART 2

The Tulip Rug

CHART 2   The Tulip Rug

CHART 2   The Tulip Rug

JUTE   4s (See Materials, Note 1, page 12)
WIDTH   36″, 143 stitches (jute = 144, 'lose' one stitch, see page 12)
LENGTH   58″ 231 stitches
Area of rug: 14½ sq. ft.
Approximate weight of wool required: 7¼ lbs.

A Portuguese rug admired at the Victoria and Albert Museum suggested the tulip motif as a basis of this design.

Stitches recommended

Surrey stitch or Turkey knot short pile.

Colour suggestions

1. Shades of brown for all dividers, outlines of meander, and large medallion and its subsidiary corners.
2. Two contrasting colours for the tooth edges.
3. The meander stalks and the lower part of the flowers could be in two shades of the same colour, the flowers being the lighter of the two. Shading in the points of the flowers indicates that a strong contrasting colour (or shade) should be used here.
4. Whatever colour (preferably in several shades) is selected for the meander border background and main background of the rug, that of the four tulip corners and large medallion should be lighter in tone than this.
5. Off-whites would be the best choice for the interior rows between the brown outlines of the large medallion and of the four tulip corners.
6. Four different shades are used to show where there should be a definite colour change within the same outline (e.g. see 3 above). Personal taste and initiative will indicate ideas for the small background motifs.

Tudor Rose Design

Size of design: 112 by 174 stitches

For a rug – 5s canvas, 27″ wide 134 stitches

To the design as charted a 9-stitch wide plain border should be added outside the 2-stitch divider shown, with another 2-stitch wide divider at the edges of the rug, thus adding 22 stitches to the width and length of the rug as charted (see Bayeux Rug, page 48).

The finished rug size will be 27″ by 39″ (134 by 196 stitches).

For a church stall seat – cut from 7″ linen canvas.

Finished size as charted will be 17″ by 26″.

Suggested: tent stitch outlines, long-legged cross stitch background, rice stitch for the border.

CHART 3   The Highway of the Sun Rug

CANVAS   5s, open mesh
WIDTH   22″, 109 stitches
LENGTH   36″, 179 stitches
Area of rug: 5½ sq. ft.
Approximate weight of wool required: 2¾ lbs.

JUTE   4s (See Materials, Note 1, page 12)
WIDTH   27″, 109 stitches
LENGTH   45″, 179 stitches
Area of rug: 8¼ sq. ft.
Approximate weight of wool required: 4¼ lbs.

This design makes use of stylised trees, here utilised as decoration for a Roman pavement laid about two thousand years ago.

In 1963, during the construction of the Autostrada del Sole in Italy, archaeological remains of particular interest and importance were brought to light at Lucus Feroniae, about twenty miles south of Rome. This was a famous religious, commercial and military centre at the time of Augustus, 63 B.C.–A.D. 14. The discoveries included statues, buildings and a vast mosaic pavement, 7,300 sq. ft. in size, a minute part of which forms the basis of this rug.

The author was recently told that the Romans used to speak of their pavements as 'economical carpets', and it would be interesting to know at what date carpets from the East which embodied these stylised trees reached Rome, where they were probably seen by one of the architects of Lucus Feroniae, and incorporated in the pavement he was designing.

Stitches recommended
Surrey stitch or Turkey knot short pile.

Colour suggestions
1. The dividers, tree outlines and field pattern (i.e. all that is printed black on the chart) – the darkest possible shade of brown, blue or red, or dark grey.
2. The trees themselves – a slightly lighter shade of their outline colour.
3. The background of the trees, and the whole of the field except the field pattern (see above) – several shades of off-white.

CHART 4

An Economy Rug

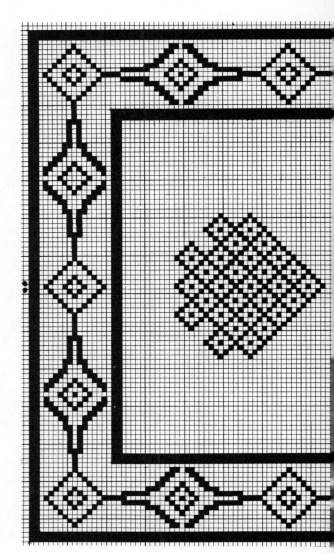

CANVAS   5s, open mesh
WIDTH   22″, 109 stitches
LENGTH   38″, 191 stitches
Area of rug: 5¾ sq. ft.
Approximate weight of wool required:
2¼ lbs.

JUTE   4s (See Materials, Note 1,
page 12)
WIDTH   27″, 109 stitches
LENGTH   48″, 191 stitches
Area of rug: 9 sq. ft.
Approximate weight of wool required: 4½ lbs.

    This is what Mrs Beeton would call a 'using up of cold remains' rug and is definitely designed for making use of 'left over' wool.

Stitches recommended
    Surrey stitch or Turkey knot short pile.

Colour suggestions
    Should the accumulated 'left overs' from many bundles of mixed thrums include (as is probable) a jumble of rather unattractive colours, these, if dyed, say, various fawns and browns, should emerge as a most useful collection of different shades and be invaluable for backgrounds.

For this rug use very dark shades as outlines for the small squares that make up the pattern in the field, medium shades for the border background and lighter shades haphazardly for the background of the field.

There are sure to be some short lengths of bright colours in the wool-bag, and these, sorted and used judiciously for the little squares of the pattern, should produce an attractive, jewel-like result.

The edging-stitch, dividers (two stitches wide each side of the border) and the outlines of the border design should be in a strong colour as a contrast to the indeterminate background – dark blue would be effective. The interiors of the border motifs could be in alternate soft colours chosen to tone with the outline or in a soft shade of the outline colour itself.

CHART 5   A One Motif Rug

CANVAS   5s, open mesh
WIDTH   22″, 109 stitches
LENGTH   38″, 193 stitches
Area of rug: 6 sq. ft.
Approximate weight of wool required: 2¼ lbs.

JUTE   4s (See Materials, Note 1, page 12)
WIDTH   27″, 109 stitches
LENGTH   48″, 193 stitches
Area of rug: 9 sq. ft.
Approximate weight of wool required: 4½ lbs.

This design is particularly simple and easy to follow, the main border pattern and the motifs in the field being closely allied, while the colour blocks that form the subsidiary borders should present no difficulty.

Stitches recommended
Surrey stitch or Turkey knot short pile.

Colour suggestions
1. Background throughout – several shades of a rather dark neutral colour are visualised for both border and field background, e.g. browns or fawns.
2. Edging-stitch and border dividers – dark blue.
3. Borders and field decoration – these should be in bright contrasting colours against the neutral background:
    (*a*) Main border – the pattern outline medium blue, the interior of the motifs orange (this arrangement of colour being reversed in all six motifs in the field of the rug), and a bright green for the crosses throughout.
    (*b*) Narrow borders – the above colours should be used alternately for the colour blocks indicated by the shading, i.e. green, medium or light blue, orange, dark blue, repeated.

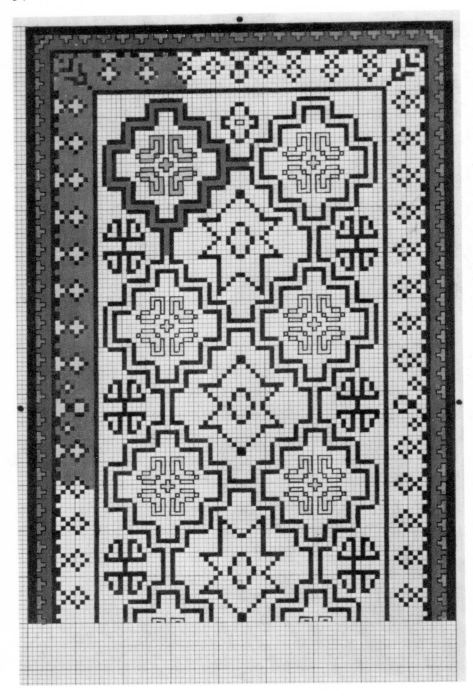

Rug designed by Mrs M. Russell, Cambridge.

CHART 6   A Repeating Design

CANVAS   5s, open mesh
WIDTH   18″, 90 stitches (canvas=89 stitches, 'gain' one stitch, see page 12)

This design can be utilised in two ways:
1. As an ordinary rug, when, having reached the centre point of the present length (shown by a black spot), the chart should be reversed and the pattern continued in the usual way until it reaches the final border.
The other measurements will then be:
LENGTH   33″, 166 stitches
Area of rug: $4\frac{1}{4}$ sq. ft.
Approximate weight of wool required: $1\frac{1}{2}$ lbs.

2. As a runner, when it can be any length desired. In this case care must be taken regarding the turning-point of the final border, which must be adjusted so that the four corners shall be alike – see Explanatory Notes, Canvas, 5, page 13.
The other measurements will then be:
LENGTH   Indefinite
Area of rug: $4\frac{1}{2}$ sq. ft. per yard run
Approximate weight of wool required: $1\frac{3}{4}$ lbs. per yard run

Stitches recommended
Surrey stitch or Turkey knot short pile.

Colour suggestions
1. The border dividers and all the outlines shown black on the chart should be in dark brown.
2. Four different shades indicate four contrasting colours that could be used. It is suggested that the narrow border stripe should be blue and red and the wider one blue and yellow.
3. The background of the medallions which have shaded patterns within them should be of a different colour or shade from the rest of the background.

CHART 7

A Small Slip-Mat

CANVAS   5s, open mesh
WIDTH   18″, 90 stitches (canvas = 89, 'gain' one stitch, see page 12)
LENGTH   41″, 204 stitches
Area of rug: $5\frac{1}{4}$ sq. ft.
Approximate weight of wool required: 2 lbs.

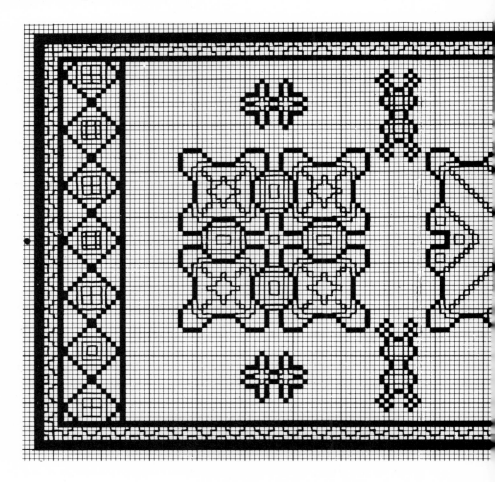

An interesting and unusual texture was achieved in this little rug by using deep long-legged cross-stitch in conjunction with long-legged cross-stitch as the background for the field.

Stitches used

Cross-stitch, long-legged cross-stitch and deep long-legged cross-stitch.

Colours used

1. Edging-stitch and dividers – chestnut-brown.
2. Narrow border – two shades of orange-brown, alternating with fawn.
3. Background of field, of end borders and of corners of medallions – in shades of fawn.
4. The two outer medallions and end border patterns – dark blue outlines.
5. Centre medallion, outline and diagonal lines dark red, large wide Vs in two shades of blue.
6. Small motifs in the field and inner patterns of the medallions and end borders – different shades of the above colours plus a small amount of green.

Designed and worked by Bishop and Mrs Cockin, Marlborough.

CHART 8   An Idea From a Greek Shoulder-Bag

CANVAS   5s, open mesh
WIDTH   22″, 109 stitches
LENGTH   37″, 187 stitches
Area of rug: $5\frac{1}{2}$ sq. ft.
Approximate weight of wool required: $2\frac{1}{4}$ lbs.

This design is based upon that of a Greek shoulder-bag which was bought on an Hellenic cruise.

Stitches recommended

1. Long-legged cross-stitch for the dividers and the background of the seven main stripes.
2. Rice stitch for the chequer patterns and the squares in the two end stripes.
3. Cross-stitch for the zigzag borders.
4. Double-cross rice stitch for the pattern in the two borders formed of 'rolling-pins' and squares and for the centre squares of the three main borders.

Colour suggestions

The background of the broad bands should be the colour that is to predominate and this should also be used for the edging-stitch throughout the rug.

Design and colour suggestions by Miss Rosalind Ord, Marlborough.

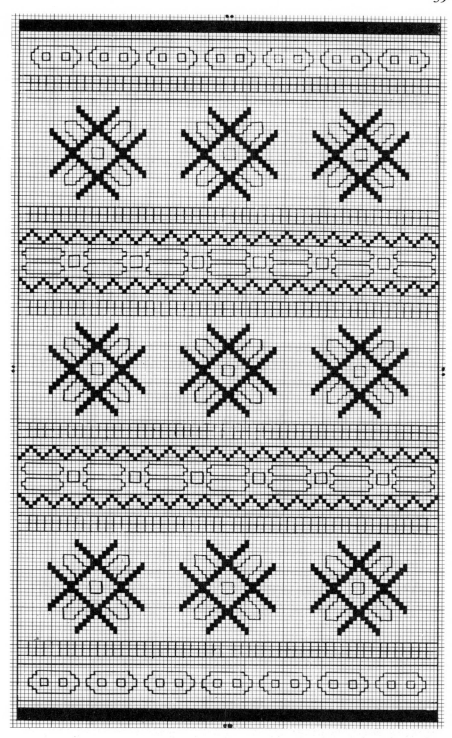

CHART 9   An Idea From a Turkish Shoulder-Bag

CANVAS   5s, open mesh
WIDTH   22″, 108 stitches (canvas = 109, 'lose' one stitch, see page 12)
LENGTH   38″, 190 stitches
Area of rug: 5¾ sq. ft.
Approximate weight of wool required: 2½ lbs.

This design is based upon that of a Turkish shoulder-bag which was bought on an Hellenic cruise.

Stitches recommended

1. Rice stitch for the narrow plain stripes, i.e. over a square of 4 all along the 2-stitch-wide rows.
2. Double-cross rice stitch for the wider plain stripes where there is a square of 9 all along the 3-stitch-wide rows.
3. Long-legged cross-stitch for the two arrow-like borders, and for the four dividers at each end of the rug.
4. Cross-stitch for the rest of the rug.

Colour suggestions

The original bag had an attractive colour scheme of cream, orange, brown and two shades of green, but any scheme of five or six colours could be effective. This is a design where personal taste and colour experiments can ensure much interest for the worker of the rug.

The predominating colour should be used for the edging-stitch throughout the rug.

Design and colour suggestions by Miss Rosalind Ord, Marlborough.

CHART 10   A Stair-Carpet

CANVAS   5s, open mesh
WIDTH   22", 109 stitches
LENGTH   Indefinite

Area of rug: $5\frac{1}{2}$ sq. ft. per yard run
Approximate weight of wool required: 2 lbs. per yard run

This rug is primarily designed as a repeating pattern for a stair-carpet but it could be used equally well as a small rug, the corners of the borders being easily adjusted for any length.

Motifs from an Oriental rug gave ideas for the co-ordinated design.

Stitches recommended

For a stair-carpet smooth-faced stitches are advised, preferably a combination of cross-stitch and long-legged cross-stitch. For an ordinary rug Surrey stitch or Turkey knot short pile could be used according to preference.

Colour suggestions

1. Edging stitch and dividers – dark brown.
2. Alternating, four colour borders – red, green, stone, blue.
3. Central border – two contrasting colours, e.g. dark blue and red.
4. Field of the rug – two or three shades of dark blue.
5. Outlines of the three continuous main motifs – stone.
6. Interior of these motifs – dark red for the outer part of the pattern, light red for the inner part.
7. The joining squares – light red with the small central crosses in green.
8. Outlines of the secondary motifs (in pairs) – light red, with stone for the filling.

This design lends itself to many different colour combinations of which the above is merely an example.

Design and colour suggestions by Miss Rosalind Ord, Marlborough.

CHART 11   An Interlacing Pattern Rug

CANVAS   5s, open mesh
WIDTH   22″, 108 stitches (canvas = 109, 'lose' one stitch, see page 12)
LENGTH   35″, 178 stitches
Area of rug: 5½ sq. ft.
Approximate weight of wool required: 2 lbs.

Stitches recommended

A smooth-faced rug is suggested for this design, the main stitches to be long-legged cross-stitch and cross-stitch.

Rice stitch or deep long-legged would be satisfactory for the 2-stitch outside divider, and rice stitch would give interest to the texture if used in the centres of the border interlace and also in the eight squares in each diagonal of the four corners.

Colour suggestions

To be effective the main border should have a light ground with the interlacing pattern worked in two different colours of a rich tone.

The 'floral'-type pattern of the narrow border could have a dark background of the same colour as the field. This colour will be the predominating colour of the whole rug.

The centre panel should again have the light ground and the same colours as the interlacing border.

All the various colours can be used in the bands across the corners.

CHART 12 — A Balkan Design

CANVAS   5s, open mesh
WIDTH   27″, 135 stitches (canvas = 134, 'gain' one stitch, see page 12)
LENGTH   43″, 217 stitches
Area of rug: 8 sq. ft.
Approximate weight of wool required: 3 lbs.

A very finely worked small pochette brought by a friend from the Balkans suggested the idea for this rug, which is not as complicated to work as it looks at first sight.

Stitches recommended
     Surrey stitch or Turkey knot short pile.

Colour suggestions
1. Dividers and outlines of the main motifs in the field – dark brown.
2. Single-stitch zigzags in the field – chestnut brown.
3. Background of the field – gold in two or more near shades.
4. Interior of field motifs – two shades of red in alternating motifs.
5. Centres of field motifs – light gold with green for the small crosses in the centre.
6. Narrow borders – chestnut-brown and green.
7. Wide border – chestnut motifs on a gold background.
Shading has been used to indicate and clarify the colour changes.
     When the centre stitch (marked by two dots), has been reached the chart should be reversed in order to complete the rug.

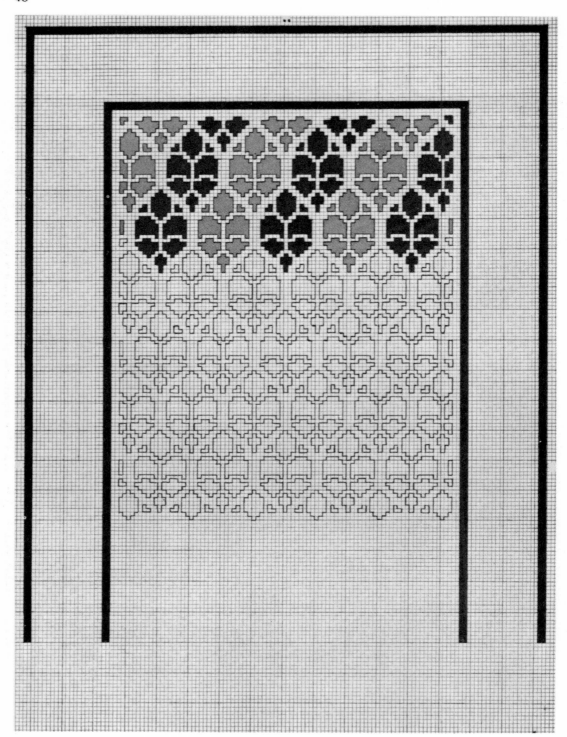

CHART 13   # The Bayeux Rug

CANVAS   5s, open mesh
WIDTH   27″, 133 stitches (canvas = 134, 'lose' one stitch, see page 12)
LENGTH   Indefinite
Area of rug: $6\frac{3}{4}$ sq. ft. per yard run
Approximate weight of wool required: $2\frac{1}{2}$ lbs. per yard run

The idea of this rug came into being via the discovery of an old picture postcard which showed clearly the lovely shapes of the stonework of a window in Bayeux Cathedral and conjured up memories of medieval stained glass.

This is a 'line' rug where the different parts of the design have not been outlined separately, as they are in the majority of the charts, the stone background itself providing the outlines for the windows. It will be noted that each window of the repeating pattern consists of eight panes of 'glass'.

Stitches recommended

1. Deep long-legged cross-stitch for the inner and outer border outlines.
2. Rice stitch and long-legged cross-stitch in a pattern for the wide, plain border or long-legged cross-stitch only if preferred.
3. Long-legged cross-stitch for background and cross-stitch for the 'stained-glass windows' or vice versa according to personal taste.

Colour suggestions

1. Field – two shades of a deep stone colour for the background and two contrasting colours for the 'windows', arranged either vertically or diagonally, as shown by the shading on the chart.
2. Border – several shades of one of the colours used in the field. It is advisable that the general tone of the border should be rather darker than that of the field.

CHART 14

Rug designed and worked by Mrs E. M. Gibson, West Hartlepool.

The Goblets Rug

CHART 14   The Goblets Rug

CANVAS   5s, open mesh
WIDTH   27″, 134 stitches
LENGTH   51½″, 258 stitches, charted 240
Area of rug: 9¾ sq. ft.
Approximate weight of wool required: 3¾ lbs.

Goblets in various forms appear frequently in Oriental rugs and they are used here in pairs as the main border stripe. Note how the corner motif in the border is repeated in the field to co-ordinate the whole design.

Stitches recommended

Long-legged cross-stitch for all backgrounds, rice stitch where there is a square of 4 on the chart (as in the pattern of the three centre medallions), double-cross rice stitch where there is a square of 9 on the chart (as in the corner motifs of the border), and cross-stitch to fill up any gaps.

Colours used – dark green, light green, lime-green; dark and light shades of orange; dark brown and off-whites.

1. Dividers and outlines of motifs – dark brown.
2. Centres of narrow border stripes – dark and light green alternately.
3. Wide border background – dark green.
4. Wide border – goblets, two shades of orange; motifs between the goblet cups, lime-green; corner motifs of border, light orange.
5. Background – outer field and interior of the three central medallions, light green; interior of large medallion, dark green.
6. Centre of the medallion outlines – off-white.

   Using the above colours, ideas for the motifs are left to individual taste.

   Shading has been used to indicate and clarify the colour changes.

   One end border has been omitted and can be copied easily be reversing the chart.

CHART 15   Coal-Chute Rug

CANVAS   5s, open mesh
WIDTH   27″, 133 stitches (canvas = 134, 'lose' one stitch, see page 12)
LENGTH   42″, 211 stitches
Area of rug: 8 sq. ft.
Approximate weight of wool required: 3 lbs.

Many people who walk along Wimpole Street appreciate the charm of the early-nineteenth-century houses but maybe do not realise that an added attraction is to be found in the covers of the coal-chutes on the pavements.

Being a frequent visitor to the Embroiderers' Guild office, I have many times visualised the possibilities of these covers forming embryonic rug designs, but the opportunity of sitting on a camp-stool with pencil and paper (the necessary preliminary) never seemed to arrive. The Guild was more enterprising and a few years ago Mrs Pilcher, an enthusiastic member, worked out six designs from the coal-covers and these were reproduced as embroidery transfers from which many delightful results have been evolved.

I am greatly indebted to the Guild, as will be anyone who works this rug, for giving kind permission to use two of these transfers to make the main basis of this design. Both transfers have been printed on page 54 to show their original form.

It is intended that one or other of these two central motifs should be used as a pair (unless a worker prefers an asymmetrical design as at present shown), but if a long strip rug is needed alternating circles would be attractive.

The spaces between the concentric circles are broken up by a pattern of lines, in which respect they differ from the similar spaces in the Roman pavement design, Charts 18A and B.

Stitches recommended
Surrey stitch or Turkey knot short pile.

54

Colour suggestions

1. Dividers – the divider line touching the edging-stitch and the one touching the field could be of a darker shade than the other four which touch the tooth edges, e.g. two shades of brown.
2. Tooth edges – two contrasting colours.
3. Main border:
   (*a*) Background – a slightly darker shade than the main field of the rug.
   (*b*) Motifs – two of the same colours used in the circular designs in the field could be

CHART 15

Coal-Chute Rug

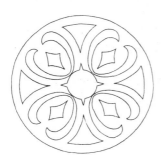

utilised, i.e. the diamonds one colour and the oblongs another. The four corner motifs could be yet a third colour or a different shade from that of the diamonds.

4. Field background – several shades of one colour.
5. Circles – the two circles and the lines joining them dark, the spaces between these lines in two contrasting colours.
6. Central coal-chute motifs – background paler than the main field, four different colours, or shades of one colour as preferred, for the patterns – shown by shading.
7. Outer plant forms – 'heads' and stems in one colour, leaves a contrast.

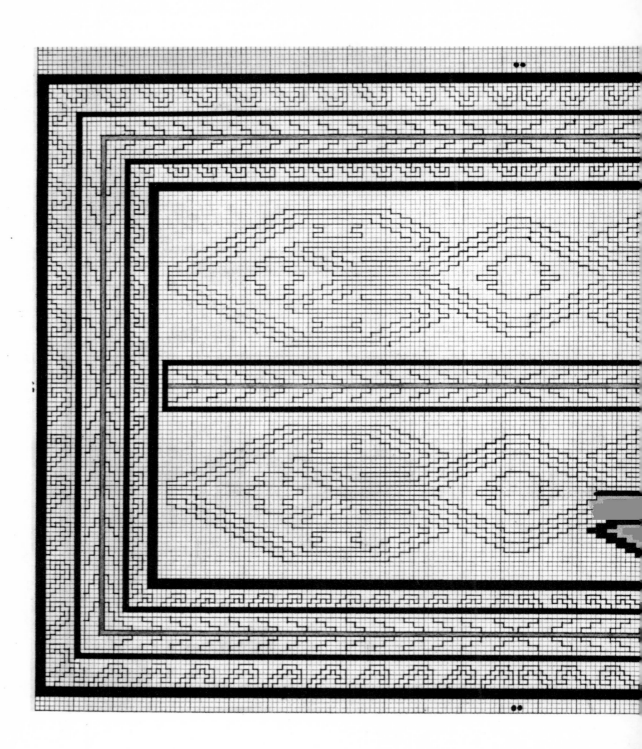

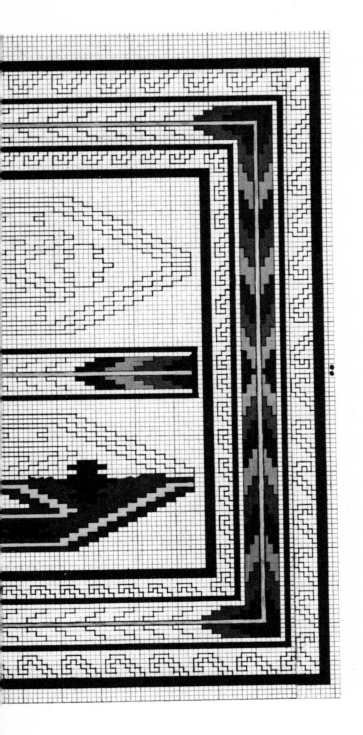

CHART 16

An Asia Minor Rug

CHART 16   An Asia Minor Rug

CANVAS   5s, open mesh
WIDTH   27", 133 stitches (canvas = 134, 'lose' one stitch, see page 12)
LENGTH   40", 199 stitches
Area of rug: 7½ sq. ft.
Approximate weight of wool required: 2¾ lbs.

The basic idea of this pattern came from a piece of woven material originating in Asia Minor and said to be towel ends.

This is a 'line' rug, i.e. the patterns on the rug are not outlined by separate stitches and rely on a clear-cut design and distinct colours to show up well.

Stitches recommended

Long-legged cross-stitch with cross-stitch where necessary.

Another name for long-legged cross-stitch is Portuguese cross-stitch, and this design offers an opportunity of experimenting by working the stitch as it is generally seen in Portugal, i.e. in different directions instead of invariably across the width of the canvas.

If this experiment is tried it is suggested that the rows of the wide outer border, its companion in the centre of the rug, and the block patterns forming the main design, should be worked lengthwise down the canvas, the rest of the design being worked backwards and forwards across the width as usual.

This idea is put forward because the design lends itself particularly well to this treatment – it is not advocated for long-legged cross-stitch as a general rule.

Colour suggestions

The stripes need to be worked in bright, clear colours to emphasise the pattern. The background of the field should be neutral in tone, e.g. blue-grey.

Shading has been used to show changes of colour.

CHART 17   # The Pineapple Rug

The tufted tops of the branching leaf forms led to the name of this rug.

The original rug was a 'baby' Soumak, worked many years ago as a teaching sampler on 10s canvas in a mixture of Brussels thrums and crewel wool. Its chief object was to illustrate the possibilities of the use of very few colours and many shades of these. In this case there were only four colours, blues and golds alternating for the background and pattern of both the border and field of the rug, with browns for the outlines and dividers and touches of cerise.

As the rug has been a popular design, a reproduction on 5s canvas has been included, for which the working figures are:

CANVAS   5s, open mesh
WIDTH   27″, 135 stitches (canvas = 134, 'gain' one stitch, see page 12)
LENGTH   49″, 247 stitches
Area of rug: $9\frac{1}{4}$ sq. ft.
Approximate weight of wool required: $3\frac{1}{2}$ lbs.

Stitches recommended

Surrey stitch or Turkey knot short pile or Soumak stitch (gain one stitch from each selvedge).

Colour suggestions

Adopting the original idea of four colours to the plan of this rug, there are many possibilities, browns being used as above.

A friend who liked the design produced a version of it where two shades of claret and other reds took the place of the blues, and many off-whites the place of the golds. A particularly attractive green-blue was introduced into the border and some of the sections of the flower centre-piece. The border itself was completely different, being more elaborate and showing less background.

60

Another suggestion would be to use a bright green in combination with a peacock-green-blue for the leaves, stone in various shades for the background and a variety of different blends of the colours for the flower sections.

Note that a 'spot' border has been introduced as an alternative to the inside two-row divider.

When the centre stitch, marked by two dots, has been reached, the chart should be reversed in order to complete the rug.

CHART 18   Roman Pavement Rug – Verulamium

CANVAS   5s, open mesh
WIDTH   27″, 135 stitches (canvas = 134, 'gain' one stitch, see page 12)
LENGTH   49½″, 247 stitches
Area of rug: 9¼ sq. ft.
Approximate weight of wool required: 3½ lbs.

If, instead of an ordinary rug, the design is used to make a long hall or landing carpet, the area will be 6¼ sq. ft., and the approximate amount of wool required 2½ lbs. per yard run.

Roman remains which have been excavated and preserved in Britain are legion, and at many sites mosaic pavements will be found which provide a particularly rewarding inspiration for the rug designer. These pavements are often the flooring of baths, and a list of good examples of these is given below. Very many of the designs have an 'interlace' surround, sometimes simple, sometimes elaborate, which is derived from a design found on very ancient pottery of which the date and place of origin is unknown.

The design charted is based upon the pavement in the baths at Verulamium (St Albans), except the Pear motif which can be seen at King's Weston Park, Bristol, and the probable date of which is the late third century A.D.

There are two ways in which this design can be utilised – as a normal rug of two motifs using either the Pear pattern in both squares or two of the Verulamium motifs, or as a long hall or landing carpet using the three Verulamium motifs alternately. The version which appears on the book's cover is being worked on 7s canvas 36 inches wide, hence the wider border and the extra panel in its width. This rug is planned for a passage 12 feet long, and when finished will have eleven pairs of the central circular or 'plate' designs, of which there will be eight variants, all based largely on the Verulamium pavement.

Stitches recommended
1. Long-legged cross-stitch for all the straight dividers.
2. Double-cross rice stitch for the 3-stitch-wide rows between the above.

   Note. Depending on the count, it often happens that there is a small gap left at the end of the row when using these large stitches, as will be seen with 2 above. The golden rule is to fill in these gaps with ordinary cross-stitch – or the cross-stitches can be put in the centre of a row if preferred, see medallion squares. A little experience will soon indicate how best to deal with this small problem.
3. Cross-stitch for the interlace outlines, the outlines of all the medallion patterns, and for the leaves in the four corners of the squares.
4. Long-legged cross-stitch everywhere else.

Colour suggestions
1. Edging-stitch and all dividers – dark brown.
2. Interlace – contrasting colours should be used to distinguish each of the bands of the interlace, and each band should be outlined in a darker shade of its own colour, or two more contrasting colours could be used. With the interlace being bright it would be advisable for the background to be a neutral colour, such as several shades of fawn.
3. Background of the large squares and of the interior of the circles – a pale yellowish green. Brussels thrums might be useful here as strands of different shades could be worked together to produce general shading and there is no reason why it should not be used in conjunction with 2-ply thrums.
4. Circles – a soft yellow outlined in deep blue. These circles are important to the design and need to show up well.
5. The centre motifs are shaded to show different colours, and each one should be outlined in a darker shade of its own colour.
6. The leaves in the corners of the squares – two shades of red.

SOME ROMAN PAVEMENTS ON DISPLAY

In situ	*In Museums*
Aldborough, West Riding	Bath, Roman Baths Museum
Bignor Roman Villa, Sussex	British Museum
Chedworth Roman Villa, Glos.	Cirencester
King's Weston Park, Bristol (Roman buildings)	Colchester
Lullingstone Roman Villa, Kent	Gloucester
Northleigh Roman Villa, Oxon.	Leeds
Verulamium (St Albans), Herts.	Leicester
	Salisbury
	Taunton

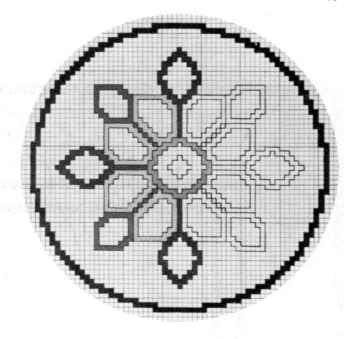

See also next page

CHART 18

Roman Pavement Rug

CHART 19A

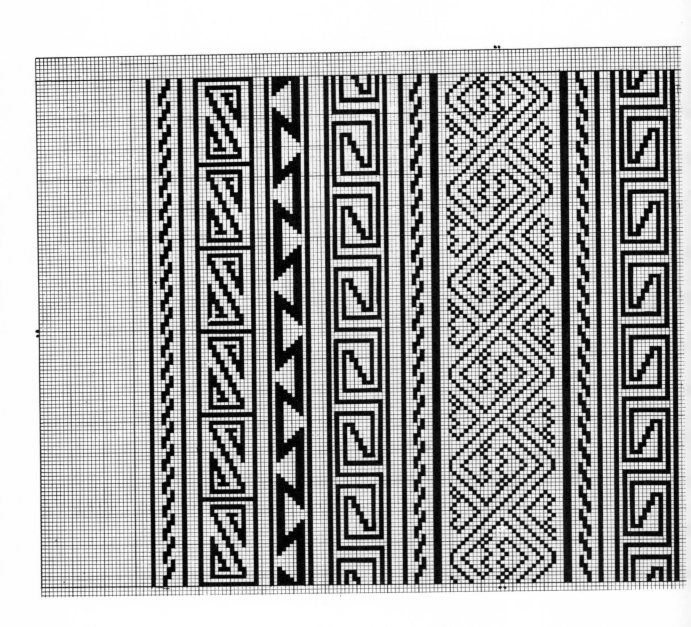

The Colorado Rug

19B

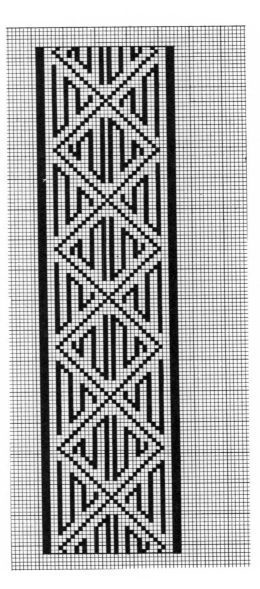

CHART 19A & B   # The Colorado Rug

CANVAS   5s, open mesh
WIDTH   27″, 133 stitches (canvas=134, 'lose' one stitch, see page 12)
LENGTH   47″, 235 stitches
Area of rug: $8\frac{3}{4}$ sq. ft.
Approximate weight of wool required: $3\frac{1}{2}$ lbs.

A postcard of unknown source formed the basis of this design. On the card were patterns, said to have been found on pottery discovered in Colorado, which dated from the thirteenth century. A striped tendency in the patterns probably meant that they had been used as decorations round large jars. The majority of the stripes as developed for this design should be easy to work, but as the wide central pattern was somewhat complicated, a second version of this has been charted and is shown, in exactly the same width, as a separate unit (19B).

Stitches recommended

Three completely different stitch ideas can be used for this design:
1. If the design is worked as charted, long-legged cross-stitch, with cross-stitch for the central stripe.
2. The design lends itself ideally to Soumak stitch as, if the second version of the central stripe is used, the whole design can be worked with particular ease across the width of the canvas, using Brussels thrums preferably.

     With Soumak the full 134 double bars of the canvas will be required, since Soumak always needs one more stitch in the width of the canvas than is shown on the chart.
3. Using the second version of the central stripe either of the short-pile stitches would suit this design.

For the 24-stitch-wide plain border at each end of the chart interlocking Gobelin stitch or deep long-legged cross-stitch would make a good contrast to the other stitches.

Colour suggestions

The stripes seem to demand a combination of brilliant colouring such as that found on Indian blankets, with a neutral colour for all the narrow stripes between the patterns. It should be noted that the latter vary in width. This variation produces a far more interesting effect than if they had all been of the same size. The wide end borders should be slightly darker than the general tone of the rug.

These corner motifs can be used as decoration for small church kneelers or alternatively for slip mats.

Obviously all four corners of the kneeler/mat should be worked in one of the designs only, the borders being extended to surround it according to the size required.

Stitch suggestions: cross stitch, long-legged cross stitch, rice stitch are all suitable, with possibly a small amount of tent stitch in the corner patterns and rows of padded satin stitch for the long dividers if using the design for kneelers.

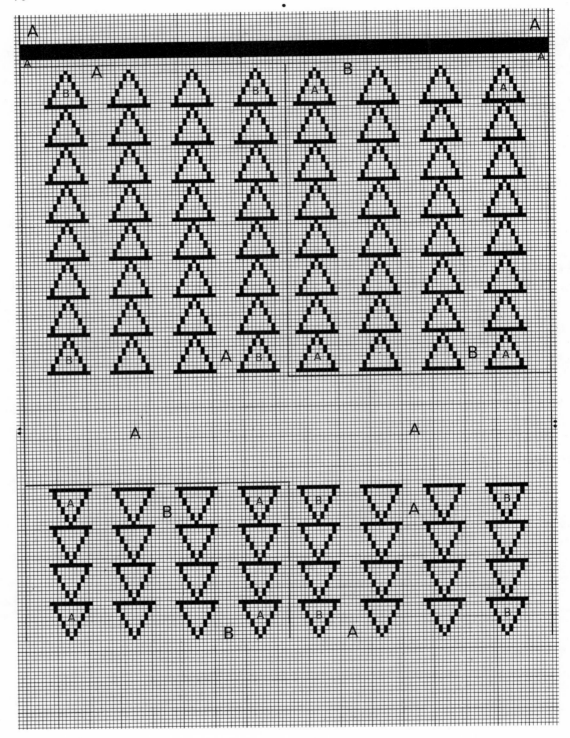

CHART 20 — A Persian 'Tree' Design

CANVAS   5s, open mesh
WIDTH   27″, 134 stitches
LENGTH   44″, 219 stitches
Area of rug: 8¼ sq. ft.
Approximate weight of wool required: 3¼ lbs.

These 'trees', taken from a Bokhara rug and used in Chart 3 page 29 as well as for this counterchange design, have already been mentioned in the Introduction. For producing an extremely simple but effective pattern nothing could be more satisfying than these little cones, which can, of course, be utilised in numerous ways apart from that here illustrated.

Stitches recommended

Interlocking Gobelin or rice stitch for the fourteen rows of 'platform' before the Tree pattern starts; cross-stitch for the outlines of the trees; long-legged cross-stitch for the interior of the trees and for the background.

Colour suggestions

This rug was designed for three colours only – a slightly pinky off-white for the outlines of the trees and for the rows of the end borders indicated by a 4-stitch-wide black line; deep indigo and a blue-red for the counterchange colour and whichever of these colours is preferred for the end borders.

The edging-stitch colour must follow that of the counterchange along the length of the rug.

To clarify – the colour A = the indigo used for the background of two sections of the tree design, for the rows forming the wide central stripe and for the trees themselves where the background changes to B (red).

B = the red used for the background of the other two sections of the design and for the trees themselves where the background is A (indigo).

It will be noted that there are only 'line' dividers between the end borders and the start of the tree pattern and also between the blocks of counterchange colour, i.e. there is no definite divider *stitch* between the colour blocks.

As designed the rug is envisaged as finishing after another four rows of trees have been worked followed by a repeat of the interlocking gobelin end border, but if desired it could be a repeating design and form a long rug or a stair-carpet.

CHART 21

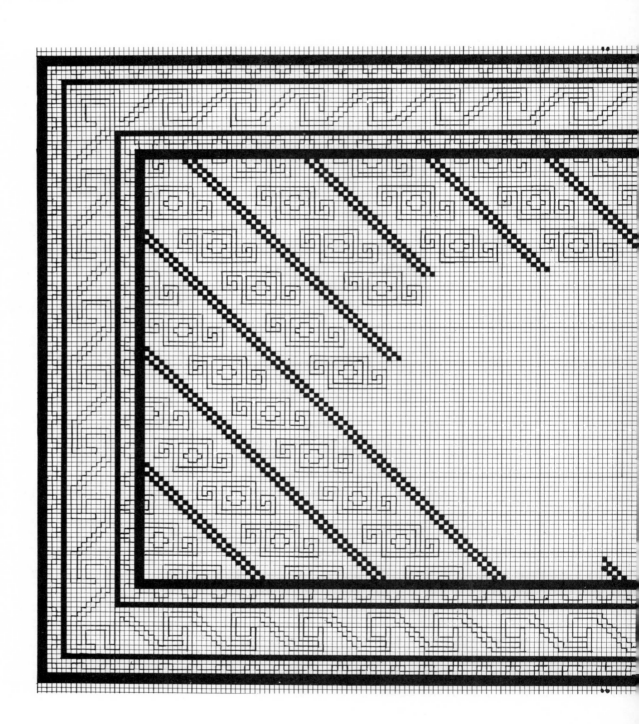

The Running Dog Rug

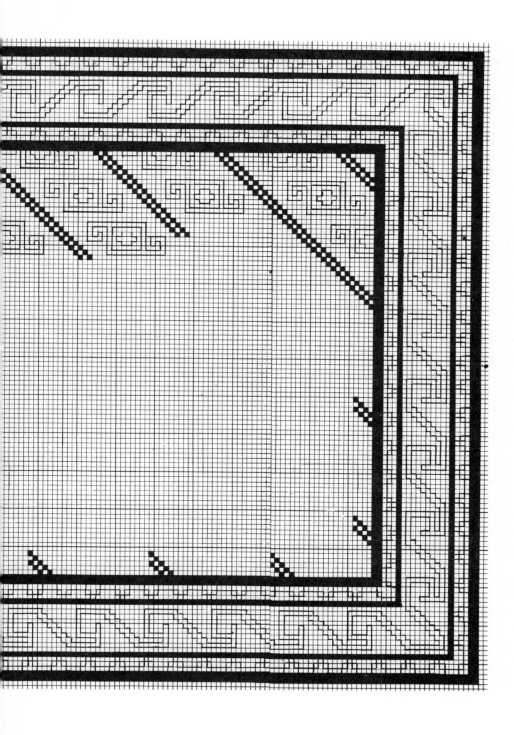

CHART 21 The Running Dog Rug

CANVAS   5s, open mesh
WIDTH   27″, 134 stitches
LENGTH   47″, 235 stitches
Area of rug: $8\frac{3}{4}$ sq. ft.
Approximate weight of wool required: $3\frac{3}{4}$ lbs.

This is an example of a 'line' rug, i.e. the motifs are not outlined as is the general practice. The decoration of this example consists mainly of patterns a single stitch wide, such as the hooks and the 'Running Dog' border. A smooth-faced rug is recommended rather than a pile, which does not do itself justice when only narrow bands of stitches are used. Both the hooks and the Running Dog pattern are often seen in Oriental rugs, the latter in numerous versions.

Stitches recommended
A combination of long-legged cross-stitch and cross-stitch.

Colour suggestions
1. The edging-stitch and the dividers throughout (both the straight lines and the out-lines of the diagonals) should be dark. The main design lends itself to bright colours which are enhanced by dark dividers.
2. The narrow borders – two contrasting colours.
3. The wide border – a medium tone background with a bright colour for the Running Dog pattern.
4. Field background. This would look very well if three different shades of one colour were selected and these shades used alternately for the different stripes.
5. Field motifs. Many variations of treatment are possible for these hooks, each of which consists of three parts. They can be worked in any combination of colours and therefore can be useful for using odds and ends of wool, or a definite colour scheme can be evolved.

CHART 22   An Oriental Type of Rug (1)

CANVAS   5s, open mesh
WIDTH   36″, 179 stitches
LENGTH   62″, 311 stitches
Area of rug: $15\frac{1}{2}$ sq. ft.
Approximate weight of wool required: $5\frac{3}{4}$ lbs.

Lack of room on the chart paper led to the omission of the second end border, which can be copied easily by reversing the chart.

This attractive rug has a particularly satisfying central medallion and is somewhat simpler than its two sisters, Charts 23 and 36.

Stitches recommended

Surrey stitch or Turkey knot short pile or Soumak stitch.

Colour notes – these are similar to those on Chart 36 with the added suggestion that the twenty-four small motifs in the field should be of a tone value very near to that of the field itself. This will give a pleasing effect of breaking up the background without making the motifs too prominent.

CHART 22

Designed by Mrs M. Russell, Cambridge.

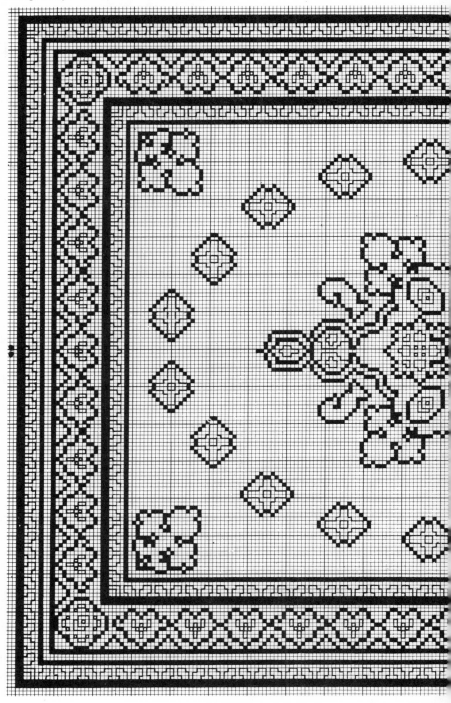

An Oriental Type of Rug (1)

CHART 23

An Oriental Type of Rug (2)

Designed by Mrs M. Russell, Cambridge.

CHART 23 An Oriental Type of Rug (2)

CANVAS   5s, open mesh
WIDTH   36″, 179 stitches
LENGTH   62″, 309 stitches
Area of rug: 15½ sq. ft.
Approximate weight of wool required: 5¾ lbs.

Lack of room on the chart paper has led to the omission of one side border. This can be copied with ease from the charted border as the rug is worked.

This design offers the advantage that it can be varied in several different ways. As an illustration, the Leaf motifs in the four square patterns in the centre of the rug could be omitted, leaving the oval medallions still linked together.

Stitches recommended

Surrey stitch or Turkey knot short pile or Soumak stitch.

Colour notes – similar to those on Chart 36.

CHART 24   An Octagonal Pattern Rug

CANVAS   5s, open mesh
WIDTH   36″, 179 stitches
LENGTH   61″, 306 stitches
Area of rug: 15¼ sq. ft.
Approximate weight of wool required: 5¾ lbs.

This Octagonal pattern is simple and interesting as, apart from the present scheme, the alternating octagons give plenty of scope for individual colouring.

Repeating designs are very restful to work and it is advised that every rug maker should have at least one such in her collection.

Stitches recommended

Surrey stitch or Turkey knot short pile.

Colour suggestions

This colour scheme bears a family resemblance to Chart 25, also designed by Miss Smith, and will make an equally attractive rug.

1. Dividers and outlines – brown (the outer row of the 3-stitch divider being worked in long-legged cross-stitch), but it is suggested that the plain row before the start of the first border should be in lime-green.
2. Background of field and widest border stripe – fawn or stone, with the latter a shade darker in tone than the field.
3. Borders:
   (*a*) Dark green and peacock-blue-green.
   (*b*) Widest border, bright blue and peacock-green alternately.
   (*c*) Lime-green and brown in a lighter tone than the dividers.
4. The colours used in the medallions, apart from their main background which is lime-green, are dark blue, peacock-blue-green and dark green, and shading has been used to indicate these colours in one of each type of medallion.

The colouring of the shaded centre medallion is: (1) dark blue between the brown outlines; (2) centre motifs, dark green between their brown outlines; (3) inner motifs filled in peacock-blue-green.

The colour scheme of the alternating medallion designs can be picked up from this shading.

One end border has had to be omitted and can be copied easily by reversing the chart.

CHART 24

Design and colour suggestions by Miss Alison M. Smith, Glasgow.

An Octagonal Pattern Rug

CHART 25

The Cats' Faces Rug

Design and colour suggestions by Miss Alison M. Smith, Glasgow.

CHART 25   # The Cats' Faces Rug

CANVAS	5s, open mesh
WIDTH	36″, 179 stitches
LENGTH	72″, 359 stitches

Area of rug: 18 sq. ft.

Approximate weight of wool required: $6\frac{3}{4}$ lbs.

Mention has been made of Hermann Haack's book, *Oriental Rugs,* and it was from one of the black and white illustrations that Miss Smith found the inspiration for this cleverly worked out repeating pattern. Hermann Haack describes the rug as having a 'pattern on a greenish gold ground giving the effect of flying eagles', but to Miss Smith the motif suggests cats' faces and other people have suggested bats. It is obviously a design that presents food for thought!

Stitches recommended

Surrey stitch or Turkey knot short pile.

Colour suggestions

There are five main colours:

1. Dividers – dark brown for the tooth-edge dividers and for the outlines of the motifs, with the exception of the narrow, inner border, for which see below, 3.
2. Background – light blue-grey throughout the field and the wide border.
3. For the outside portion of the tooth edge, half of each of the large motifs in the wide border, the dividers of the inner, narrow border and the lower part of the main field motifs – the cats' faces – bright, darkish blue.
4. The other half of the main border motif, the background of the narrow inner border and the smallest part of the main field motif – peacock-blue-green.
5. The inner half of the tooth edge, the filling of the small inner border and the central portion of the main field motifs – yellow.

A variety of colours can be used with discretion for the fillings of the small motifs scattered throughout the rug.

CHART 26   A Greek Key Pattern Design

CANVAS   5s, open mesh
WIDTH   36", 179 stitches
LENGTH   56", 281 stitches
Area of rug: 14 sq. ft.
Approximate weight of wool required: $5\frac{1}{4}$ lbs.

The borders used for this design occur in many Greek pavements as well as on vases. Care should be taken in working both the borders to follow the chart exactly, since many adjustments have been made in each to ensure that they fit the canvas satisfactorily.

Stitches recommended

1. Either rice stitch or deep long-legged cross-stitch could be used for the two-stitch-wide dividers. Rice stitch for the divider enclosing the large plain centre and deep long-legged cross-stitch for the two on each side of the Key pattern, or vice versa, would make for interest in the working.
2. Cross-stitch and long-legged cross-stitch for the rest of the pattern are an obvious choice as both are highly satisfactory when shading is necessary, as in the case of the plain central expanse.

Colour suggestions

As the Key pattern is an 'interlace' each of the lines should have different (bright to medium) colours, or shades of the same colour, between the dark coloured outlines (black on the chart). The squares should be in bright colours and the background light.

The Wave pattern should be worked in two strongly contrasting tones with the darker on the outside (one of the waves has been shaded to show the contrast). The Greeks usually used black and white for this pattern, but this is not necessary as long as there is a sharp contrast.

The centre is plain and should be worked in three or four shades of the same colour to give texture to a large, plain area.

CHART 26

Design adaptation and colour scheme by Miss Rosalind Ord, Marlborough.

A Greek Key Pattern Design

CHART 27

Design and colour suggestions by Miss Rosalind Ord, Marlborough.

The Cube Rug

CHART 27   The Cube Rug

CANVAS   5s, open mesh
WIDTH   36", 179 stitches
LENGTH   61", 305 stitches
Area of rug: 15¼ sq. ft.
Approximate weight of wool required: 5¾ lbs.

The field of this design is adapted from a Greek pavement and shows a series of cubes.
It can be worked with or without the small patterns on the top surfaces as desired.

Stitches recommended

Cross-stitch and long-legged cross-stitch, with deep long-legged cross-stitch worked
longitudinally for the wide dividers. It is particularly important that the backwards and
forwards directions of the long-legged cross-stitch should be carefully observed, as it is
vital that the meeting of the cubes should be clear cut.

Both the outlines and the fillings of the small patterns on the top of the cubes should be
in cross-stitch.

Colour suggestions

To be effective it is important that one side of the cube should be dark and the other
side light, with a medium tone on the top surface. If this is done, a very pleasant diagonal
pattern is formed by the light sides going one way and the dark sides the other. Shading
has been used to ensure clarity.

The background of the borders would look equally well if worked in either the palest
or the darkest colour used for the cubes.

The small patterns on the top of the cubes should be in a contrasting colour and the
same colour (or colours) could be used for the 'bones' on the end borders and the centres
of the small pattern in the narrow side borders.

Lack of room on the chart paper led to the omission of the second end border, which
can be copied easily by reversing the chart.

CHART 28   A Rug Design From Fiji

CANVAS   5s, open mesh
WIDTH   36″, 179 stitches
LENGTH   66″, 332 stitches (see below)
Area of rug: 16½ sq. ft.
Approximate weight of wool required: 6¼ lbs.

Owing to the size of the chart paper only 282 of the 332 stitches needed to finish the rug could be charted. When the end of the chart has been reached it should be turned round and the pattern completed.

This is a type of design that would make a most attractive long carpet and is very easy to extend.

Our greatest distances when seeking for sources of suitable designs for rugs have been Babylon in point of time and Fiji in that of mileage. On her way to Australia Miss Ord landed at Suva and in the big open market there was much attracted by a hanging, painted on bark, from which she evolved this design.

Stitches recommended

A smooth-faced rug would be best for this pattern, many alternative stitch ideas being possible, and experiments should be tried.

1. The dividers – long-legged cross-stitch.
2. Rice stitch and long-legged cross-stitch alternating for the blocks of bars in the outer border.
3. Shaded cross-stitch (preferably in off-whites) as a filling for the centre flower motifs with long-legged cross-stitch for the large, plain expanse.

Colour suggestions

The original colour scheme was very effective in black, cream and two shades of rich brown. The two browns are indicated by two shades, the lighter being that shown as the background of the centre medallion and elsewhere where the same shade is used. The remainder was black and cream, but it is advised that the darkest possible shade of red should be used as a substitute for the black. The Fijian colours were almost certainly vegetable-dyed, commercial black is generally literally dead black. Therefore, unless home-dyeing is tried, when the black will be less 'hard' – and might even have a few amateur streaks to soften it – the suggestion is made of dark red in its place.

CHART 28

Design and colour suggestions by Miss Rosalind Ord, Marlborough.

A Rug Design From Fiji

CHART 29   An Archaeological Rug

CANVAS   5s, open mesh
WIDTH   36″, 179 stitches
LENGTH   60″, 301 stitches
Area of rug: 15 sq. ft.
Approximate weight of wool required: 5¾ lbs.

Great interest in archaeology inspired this design and has resulted in a fascinating range of patterns co-ordinated to make a most attractive whole. Mrs Chisholm has had experience in archaeological 'digs' and has taken much trouble regarding the accuracy of her motifs. To add interest to the design and the finished rug she has drawn a page of archaeological finds in the 'rough' and then squared them to show how they appear on the chart.

Stitches recommended
    Surrey stitch or Turkey knot short pile.

Colours suggested
1. The edging-stitch, dividers and all outlines should be brown, except for the central row of the three-stitch dividers between the borders and the field, which should be gold.
2. The arrow-heads in the outer border – alternately dark orange and dark brown on a yellow background.
3. Zigzag border – medium green, and gold outlines on a darker green background, preferably shaded, using two or three different shades.
4. The wide inner border – outlines brown (as above), the main motifs in two shades of blue, the lighter being nearest the field, and the U-shaped joining pieces in red. For clarity, these colour changes are indicated by three different shades.
5. Dagger-hafts – three shades of gold within the brown outlines.
6. Background – as many near shades of green as possible. If there is difficulty in getting enough shades of 2-ply wool, Brussels thrums (using an adequate number of lengths) can be used combined with the 2-ply.
7. Other motifs as wished by the worker.

KEY
Pre-History Rug.

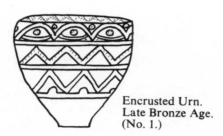

Encrusted Urn.
Late Bronze Age.
(No. 1.)

Urn from Manton. Early
Bronze Age, Wessex.

Gold Lumula,
Early Bronze Age.

(adapted)
Taken from
above Urn.

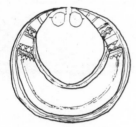

Adapted from above
Lumula.

Border – adapted from the Bronze
Age Urn above. (No. 1.)

Barbed Harpoon Heads
(Cromagnard) British Museum.

Adapted from Harpoon Head –
above.

Arrow Heads – Early Bronze Age,
Wessex.

Gold Dagger
Haft
from Bush
Barrow,
Normanton.
Used in large
centre motif of
rug.

Silver Brooch set
with amber.
British Museum.

White Horse – Uffington.

Outside Border – Arrow Heads
taken from above.

White Horse – adapted from above.

Middle Border – taken from primitive
design on above Encrusted Urn.

CHART 29

Rug designed and worked by Mrs Chisholm, Leigh, Reigate.

CHART 30

Manx Motifs

Drawn by Mrs M. Russell, Cambridge.

These interesting examples of Manx designs include adaptations of patterns found on ancient crosses in the Isle of Man.

CHART 31   Adaptation From a Herat Rug

CANVAS   7s, open mesh
WIDTH   27″, 179 stitches
LENGTH   53″, 349 stitches
Area of rug: 10 sq. ft.
Approximate weight of wool required: 3½ lbs.

This is a good example of a composite rug design. The basic pattern of the field was taken from the wide border of a Herat rug and loosely adapted to the size required. The Key pattern used for the outer of the three borders was noticed in a detail from a decorative fresco by Pontormo when browsing through Berenson's *Italian Painters of the Renaissance*. The other two borders 'just came'.

One of the attractions of the design is the effective use of the straight lines in the borders in contrast to the gracious curves of the field pattern, while the colouring of field and border keys them up with each other.

Stitches used

Cross-stitch and long-legged cross-stitch.

Colours used

1. Edging-stitch and first three dividers dark brown – other dividers dark blue.
2. Borders – blue and red with touches of off-white and lime-green.
3. Background of field – three shades of red.
4. Main pattern of field – two shades of blue with fawn outlines.

When the centre stitch, marked by two dots, has been reached, the chart should be reversed in order to complete the rug.

CHART 31

Adaptation from a Herat Rug

Designed and worked by Mr N. P. Birley, Marlborough.

CHART 32   The Ravenna Rug

CANVAS   7s, open mesh
WIDTH   28″, 189 stitches
LENGTH   46″, 301 stitches
Area of rug: 9 sq. ft.
Approximate weight of wool required: 3½ lbs.

The little town of Ravenna, left solitary in the marshes as the Adriatic receded, enshrines in her famous ancient religious buildings the miracle of her mosaics to fill with wonder those who see them.

Stepping into the Mausoleum of the Roman Empress, Galla Placidia (built in her lifetime, about A.D. 440), it seemed unbelievable that these scintillating, jewel-like mosaics could have been there for so long a time.

Nothing was more lovely and impressive than the brilliant blue vaulted ceiling studded with golden and other coloured stars, the whole effect being enhanced by the soft light coming through the translucent sheets of alabaster that took the place of glass in the windows.

The imperative wish to design a rug that would help us to retain the memory of the exquisite building was immediate, a picture postcard ensured a general recollection on our return home, and it was decided to work out a design based on the vaulted ceiling, which is an all-over repeating pattern. The pattern used for the end borders is a version of the framework of many of the mosaic 'pictures' in the Mausoleum, also in blue and gold.

No canvas coarser than 7s would be suitable for such a design, but it was felt that a repeating pattern on 36-inch-wide canvas might become somewhat monotonous so it is suggested that some of the canvas should be sacrificed and that the rug should be only 189 stitches in width. Having counted 189 double bars from one selvedge edge, the canvas should be cut after the 192nd double bar, machined up and down its length twice and then a narrow binding machined over this. Care should be taken to ensure that the result when finished is about the same width as the *uncut* selvedge.

Stitch suggestions

As this is a 'line' design the rug should be smooth-faced, and long-legged cross-stitch is advised for the background and cross-stitch for all the Star patterns. Tent-stitch would be a suitable alternative for the background, but although its shading possibilities are rather more delicate than that of long-legged cross-stitch, it takes far longer to work and the expanse of the field is quite considerable.

Colour suggestions
1. Edging-stitch – dark blue.
2. First two rows of *end border* – dark blue.
3. Gold background.
4. Blue hooks – two shades of blue.
5. Gold centre line of joined crosses.
6. Blue hooks – two shades of blue.
7. Gold background.
8. Two rows of dark blue (as for 2).
9. One row of off-white.

This finishes the end border. The field of the rug should be in two or more shades of rich blue.

Field motifs – shaded to clarify colour changes.

1. *The largest motif*
   Outer crosses and outline – gold.
   Inner single outline – dark blue.
   Diagonal crosses – blue.
   Straight T shapes – red.
   Central 5 stitch cross – gold.
   Field of circle – off-white.

2. *The medium-sized motif*
   The eight outer motifs – alternate off-white and red.
   Outline of centre – gold.
   Field of centre – off-white.
   Four 3-stitch motifs – dark blue.

3. *The smallest motif*
   The eight outer motifs – alternate off-white and red.
   Central 5-stitch cross – gold.

4. All scattered stars – various shades of gold.

The use of Brussels thrums would be particularly suitable for this design as the shading of the blues and golds is of such importance, and Brussels gives a softer effect than 2-ply thrums.

Lack of room on the chart paper led to the omission of most of the far end border. This can be copied easily by reversing the chart.

CHART 32

The Ravenna Rug

CHART 33

The Fra
Angelico Rug

Adaptation of design and colouring by
Miss Rosalind Ord,
Marlborough.

CHART 33 {style=inline} The Fra Angelico Rug

CANVAS   7s, open mesh
WIDTH   36″, 237 stitches
LENGTH   61″, 402 stitches
Area of rug: 15¼ sq. ft.
Approximate weight of wool required: 5¼ lbs.

Nearly ten years ago a kind relative said 'You two are abysmally ignorant of pictures, you need educating, we will go to Bruges.' The culminating point of that visit was being introduced to Memlinc's 'The Mystic Marriage of St Catherine', with much of a lovely rug showing beneath her feet, and since then the hunt for rugs, in conjunction with pictures by the Old Masters, has been a never-ending source of interest and entertainment.

Last year the pleasure of a visit to Florence was enhanced by discovering a rug completely different from any that we had seen before either in or out of a picture.

In the Convent of San Marco, among the exquisite Fra Angelico paintings, was one of The Virgin and Child, with a large expanse of rug to be seen under her feet, in which the field was largely covered by the most fantastic animals imaginable. We felt that Fra Angelico, having himself painted the lovely figures, must have turned to his assistants and told them to finish the subsidiary painting of the picture, and we hoped and believed that he gained amusement from what was subsequently shown to him.

Obviously these animals had to be charted, and Miss Ord, who was with us, has drawn the animals from sketches she made at the time.

There are six different animals and in order to finish the rug two pairs of these must be added beyond where the chart ends, plus, of course, the second end border. Lack of room on the chart paper led also to the omission of part of one side border, which can be copied with ease from the charted border as the rug is worked.

Stitches recommended
Surrey stitch or Turkey knot short pile.

Colour suggestions
1. On the original rug blues, greys and cream (or pale grey) predominated, among soft fawns and browns.
2. The zigzag patterns could be brown on a pale grey background, with broad bands of blue and darker grey on either side.
3. The animals should be in fawns and browns on a cream background.
4. The oak leaf border should pick up the colours of the dividing bands – brown outline, blue leaves and light grey ground.
5. The narrow border could have a pale design on a deep blue ground.

CHART 34   An Oriental Type of Rug (3)

CANVAS   7s, open mesh
WIDTH   36″, 237 stitches
LENGTH   68″, 451 stitches
Area of rug: 17 sq. ft.
Approximate weight of wool required: 6 lbs.

In order to accommodate this chart to the size of the page of the book without excessive reduction, it was necessary to omit one side border, and also part of the design beyond the centre point. The missing border can be worked without difficulty by copying in reverse the border which is charted. When the centre point has been reached, the chart should be turned round for the remainder of the working of the rug.

Stitch used

Surrey stitch short pile (Soumak stitch suitable)

Main colours used

1. The edging-stitch, the first divider, the outer rows of the other dividers, the outlines of the four corners and of the central and its subsidiary medallion, are dark brown with off-white fillings.
2. The meander of the outer border is light brown with red and blue on each side of it.
3. The background of the main border is deep blue, the motifs alternately pale blue and red, with light green or off-white centres.
4. Backgrounds:
   (*a*) Corners – light green.
   (*b*) Main field – various shades of brown (greys, off-whites, and fawns were home-dyed to produce this result).
   (*c*) Centre medallion (outer section) – green, as in the corners, or yellow could be used if preferred.
   (*d*) Inner medallion – red.

The scattered motifs are to be worked according to taste, shading showing where a definite colour contrast is indicated.

CHART 34

An Oriental Type of Rug (3)

Rug designed and worked by
Mrs I. M. Mileham, Harpenden.

CHART 35   # The Babylonian Rug

CANVAS   7s, open mesh
WIDTH   36″, 237 stitches
LENGTH   64″, 420 stitches
Area of rug: 16 sq. ft.
Approximate weight of wool required: 5½ lbs.

The end of the chart is the half-way point of the design; when this has been reached the chart should be turned round and the other half worked to complete the rug.

To most people Babylon is mainly associated with the terrifying story of the 'writing on the wall' seen by Belshazzar, grandson of Nebuchadnezzar, at his last great feast. Recent archaeological excavations on the site of the ancient city have revealed a past which fits the picture, both as regards the luxurious surroundings, and the fulfilment of the supernatural warning.

In J. D. Macqueen's book *Babylon*, a vivid description is given of a wall on the outside of Nebuchadnezzar's throne-room (built during his reign, 602–562 B.C.), which was decorated with enamelled brickwork – surely one of the earliest precursors of modern hand-painted tiles. This brickwork depicted a number of yellow columns with light blue capitals surmounted by three pairs of spiral scrolls above which were daisy-like flowers with yellow centres and white petals. Between the scrolls and joined to them by curved light blue bands, were buds in light blue, yellow and white while the main background was dark blue.

The descriptions and line-drawings of the features revealed in these excavations roused an urge to embody some of them in a rug design.

The central design on this chart is a very simplified version of a flower border which surrounded the columns. The animals below these columns appear on one of the main gates of the city and are *said* to be 'bulls' and 'dragons'. Their description mentioned that these 'dragons' had green scales and so should presumably be coloured green by anyone working the rug. It is suggested that the 'bulls' might be 'Herefords' as to colour.

The fabulous beasts that fill the end borders are said to be 'lions with snake's necks' and were taken from a drawing of a cylinder-seal found in the Babylonian region and dating from *c.* 3000 B.C.

Stitches recommended

Surrey stitch or Turkey knot short pile.

Colour suggestions

Anyone embarking upon this rug would probably like to follow at least some of the original colour ideas (used with discretion), even if only from the historical point of view. There are bound to be individual preferences and, for instance, the dark blue background would be somewhat overpowering for the border.

CHART 35

The Babylonian Rug

CHART 36

An Oriental
Type of
Rug (4)

Designed by Mrs M. Russell,
Cambridge.

CHART 36   An Oriental Type of Rug (4)

CANVAS   7s, open mesh
WIDTH   36″, 236 stitches, charted 197 (canvas = 237, 'lose' one stitch, see page 12)
LENGTH   63″, 412 stitches, charted 290
Area of rug: 15¾ sq. ft.
Approximate weight of wool required: 5½ lbs.

Lack of room on the chart paper led to the omission of part of the design, which can be copied easily by reversing the chart and picking up the design at the point marked X, and also of one of the side borders which can be copied from the charted border as the rug is worked.

This very beautiful design could be worked in two ways:

1. Exactly as it is charted.
2. As some people prefer a borderless rug the borders could be omitted and the field background continued to the edge of the canvas. The present extension of the design from the diagonal cross to the end border (16 stitches) should then be omitted.

Stitches recommended

Surrey stitch or Turkey knot short pile or Soumak stitch.

Colouring

Colour ideas are not suggested for this elaborate Oriental type of rug. It is hoped that there will be readers who would wish to evolve their own ideas, and in any case it would be impracticable to give an adequate description owing to the complexity of the design.

Before embarking on a colour scheme it is suggested that prospective workers should study the excellent coloured illustrations in Hermann Haack's book and others mentioned in the Bibliography, visit museums, historic houses (many of which are open to the public and exhibit lovely rugs among the treasures), and, if possible, borrow a good rug and browse over it at leisure.

CHART 37 Toy Soldiers Rug

CANVAS   5s, open mesh
WIDTH   22″, 109 stitches
LENGTH   41″, 204 stitches
Area of rug: $6\frac{1}{4}$ sq. ft.
Approximate weight of wool required: $2\frac{1}{2}$ lbs.

This is chiefly a 'line' rug, i.e. the majority of the motifs on the rug are not outlined by separate stitches but rely on a clear-cut design and distinct colours to show up well against the neutral background.

Stitches used

The rug is worked chiefly in long-legged cross-stitch, single cross-stitches being used in certain places, e.g. the stitch that forms the faces and hands of the soldiers, the flag-staffs, etc.

Colours used

1. Background – blue-grey throughout.
2. Edging-stitch, dividers, sentry-boxes, engine 'name-plates' – a medium-dark blue.
3. Engines – scarlet, except for the 'name-plates' (see above); wheels and couplings black. The couplings are formed by two diagonal back-stitches.
4. Signals – posts black, arms scarlet.
5. Soldiers – busbies, black; faces and hands (between busbies and tunics), white; tunics – scarlet; trousers – dark blue; guns – six black back-stitches; single odd stitches missing in trousers and tunics=background.
6. Bugles – blue and red, contrast shown by two shadings.
7. Drums – centres dark blue, crossed with lines of scarlet back-stitch running width-wise across the rug (not shown on chart); ends and sides – scarlet; sticks – blue shafts and scarlet ends.
8. Flag-staffs – brown; flags – scarlet.

CHART 37   Toy Soldiers Rug

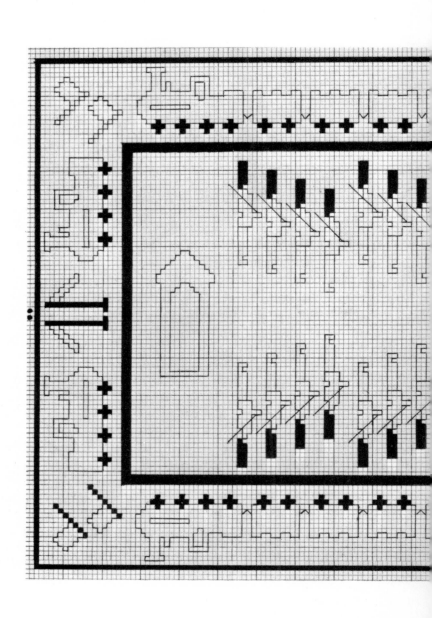

Rug designed and worked by Mrs N. Gladwin, Saltwood, Kent.

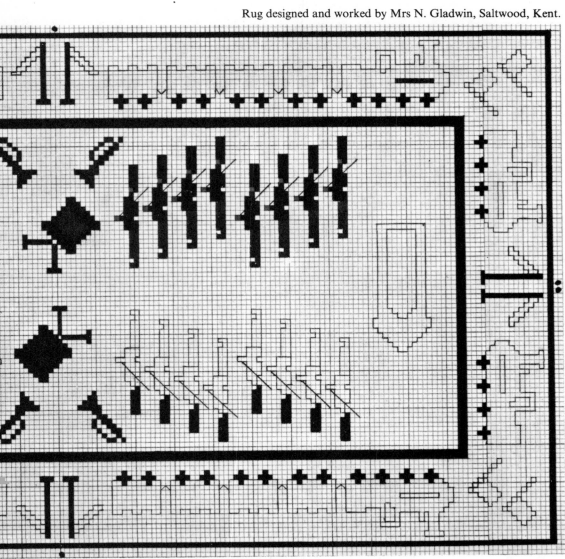

CHART 38

The Noah's Ark Rug

CHART 38   # The Noah's Ark Rug

CANVAS   5s, open mesh
WIDTH   27″, 135 stitches (canvas = 134, 'gain' one stitch, see page 12)
LENGTH   48″, 239 stitches
Area of rug: 9 sq. ft.
Approximate weight of wool required: $3\frac{1}{2}$ lbs.

Many requests for the charting of this rug have led to its reproduction exactly as it appeared in *Needle-made Rugs*, but it is hoped that individual colour schemes will be thought out by those who work it from this chart.

Stitches used

In the original, long-legged cross-stitch was used for all the dividers and the background and cross-stitch for everything else. Some of the smaller animals might, with advantage, have been worked in tent-stitch by splitting the bars of the canvas.

Colours used

1. Background – two shades of deep blue. The background had to have special treatment, see page 14 in Explanatory Notes (the Wool section).
2. Edging-stitch, dividers, outlines of animals and letters of the alphabet – deep red.
3. Mr Noah's trousers, Mrs Noah's skirt and the roof of the Ark – light red.
4. Mr and Mrs Noah's jackets and the hull of the Ark – bright green.
5. The animals – many shades of yellow and gold.
6. Mr and Mrs Noah's outline, the waves, the living-quarters of the Ark and the background of the letters of the alphabet – off-white.
7. The doors of the Ark were back-stitched in blue.
   Shading has been used to indicate and clarify the colour changes.

CHART 39   Children's Rug

CANVAS   5s, open mesh
WIDTH   36″, 179 stitches
LENGTH (finished)   65″, 325 stitches
Area of rug: 16¼ sq. ft.
Approximate weight of wool required: 6¼ lbs.

When the rug reaches the centre point of its length (indicated by one black spot) it should be reversed and the pattern continued in the usual way until the finished length is reached.

Stitches recommended

Surrey stitch short pile except for the borders, the first two rows of which should be in long-legged cross-stitch all round the rug.

Colour suggestions

1. Dark brown for the outlines of the figures and the borders.
2. Different shades of brown for the hair.
3. Cream in several shades for the broad stripes, i.e. between the rows of legs.
4. Red for the stripes between the rows of heads.
5. Two shades of blue (used alternately as stripes) for the girls' bodices and the boys' pull-overs.
6. Red 'shorts' and trousers for the boys, red stockings and socks for both boys and girls.
7. White for the faces and hands.
8. Dark brown shoes.

CHART 39

Design and colour suggestions by Miss Alison M. Smith, Glasgow.

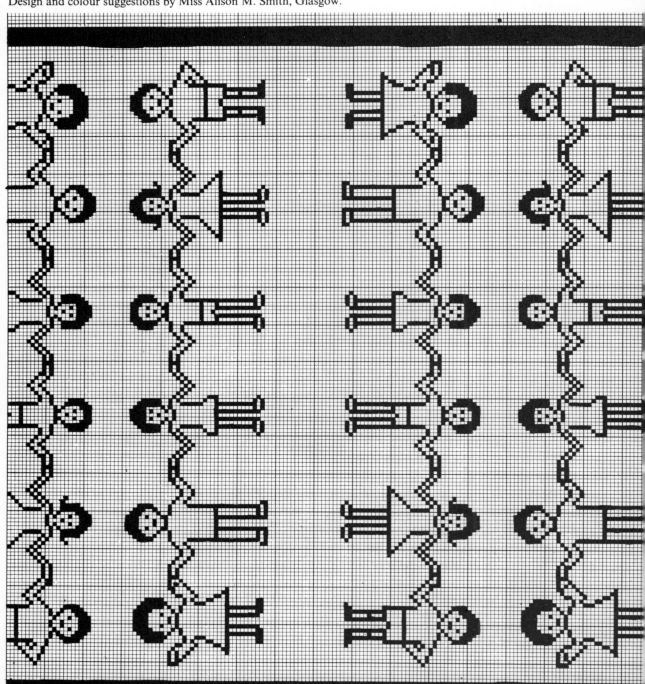

Children's Rug

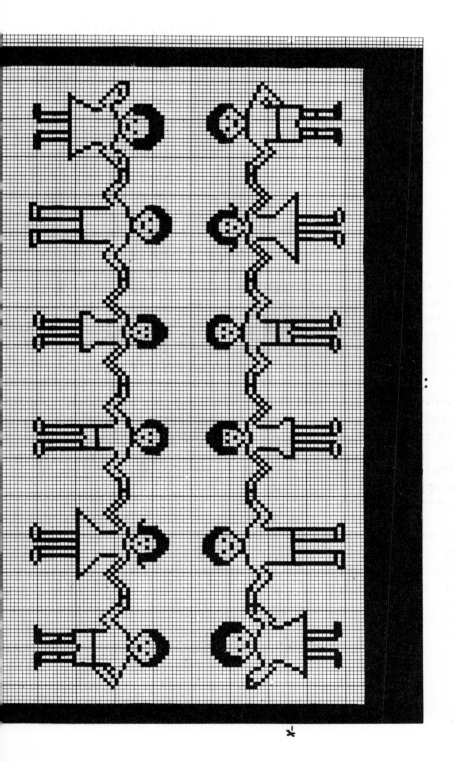

CHART 40

Animal Motifs

Small human figures and animals appear frequently in Oriental rugs, adding interest and often amusement to the designs.

This page introduces animals from four different sources and it is hoped that they may prove useful (and possibly ornamental) for space filling when invention runs out.

1. The three pairs of joined birds were found carved on Lincoln Cathedral.
2. The birds on the right of the chart and below the first group appear on Portuguese rugs.
3. The bird with wings (bottom row, second from the left), was found on a Babylonian cylinder-seal dating from *c*. 3000 B.C. – see also Chart 35, page 114.
4. The animals on the left are silhouettes of local animals which were used in a rug made some years ago.

Care should be taken that the canvas is of a suitable count for the animals selected, as if it is too coarse they will appear overpoweringly large.

The following table is given for guidance:

	10s canvas	*7s canvas*	*5s canvas*
Pair of animals, top centre	$4 \cdot 8'' \times 2 \cdot 9''$	$7'' \times 4\frac{1}{4}''$	$9\frac{1}{2}'' \times 6''$
Pair of birds back to back	$3 \cdot 7'' \times 2 \cdot 7''$	$5\frac{1}{2}'' \times 4''$	$7\frac{1}{2}'' \times 5\frac{1}{2}''$
Portuguese bird, right-hand bottom corner	$3 \cdot 7'' \times 3 \cdot 3''$	$5\frac{1}{4}'' \times 4\frac{3}{4}''$	$7\frac{1}{2}'' \times 6\frac{1}{2}''$
Small cock, next to above	$1 \cdot 2'' \times 1 \cdot 4''$	$1\frac{3}{4}'' \times 2''$	$2\frac{1}{4}'' \times 3''$
Pony, top left	$2 \cdot 2'' \times 1 \cdot 6''$	$3\frac{1}{8}'' \times 2\frac{1}{4}''$	$4\frac{1}{2}'' \times 3\frac{3}{4}''$

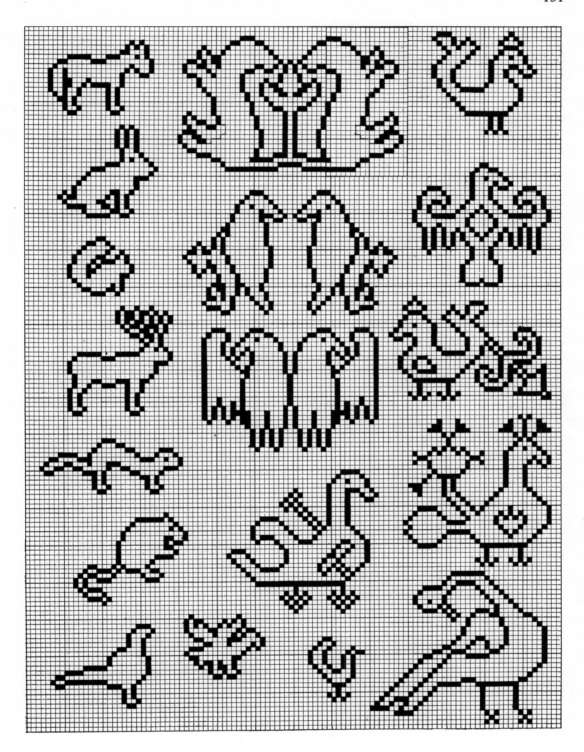

Communion Kneelers

Embarking upon a long Communion kneeler is a large project, the length of the altar rail being usually considerable and the width of the step, though varying greatly, being an average of 10 to 13 inches.

Sometimes the kneeler is worked in one piece but more often it is divided into two or more lengths and several people take part, one acting as a leader and shouldering the main responsibility for the finished work. It is obvious that this leader must be an accomplished needlewoman with a wide knowledge of stitches, methods of working, materials, quantities needed, etc.

Of the four designs charted two are 12 inches wide, one is $11\frac{1}{2}$ inches and one 10 inches, to allow for differences in step widths. It is unlikely that these will be narrower than 10 inches and a few extra rows of background could easily be added if greater width is required.

Naturally the width of canvas needed will depend on the width of the step and also on whether the kneeler is to be lined and (preferably) slightly padded, or of the mattress type.

No colour suggestions are offered as for church work the colouring depends upon the church itself, its general decorations, furnishing, glass, other embroideries *in situ* and the tastes of the individuals concerned.

As with the colouring, so with the stitches, the experts will have their own ideas on the subject. One point may be mentioned here for guidance – the Cross being of the greatest importance to all the designs, the stitches used for it should invariably aim to make this very apparent.

CHART 41 St David's Cathedral

CHART 41

A Communion Kneeler
(St David's Cathedral)

CANVAS   7s, open mesh (linen)
WIDTH   12″, 90 stitches – cut from 36″ canvas

It will be noticed that the chart is divided into three sections marked A, B and C. The length of the rug as charted is a total of the three sections, i.e.

$$
\begin{array}{ll}
\text{A} & 4\frac{1}{2}'' \\
\text{B} & 1'\ 7\frac{1}{2}'' \\
\text{C} & 1'' \\
\hline
& 2'\ 1'' \\
\hline
\end{array}
$$

For a long kneeler for the Communion rail, Section B should be repeated as often as required, but it must be remembered that room must be allowed for the beginning and end of the rug (A and C).

Four alternative designs are given for the squares surrounding the cross.

The 2 feet 1 inch combination of A, B and C above could make a stall seat cushion, any adjustments needed in size, either in length or width, being made by adding plain rows of background colour to the sides and ends.

Approximate weight of wool required per yard run: $16\frac{1}{2}$ oz.

The idea for this rug came from the magnificent Presbytery Roof of St David's Cathedral.

Details from Chart 41

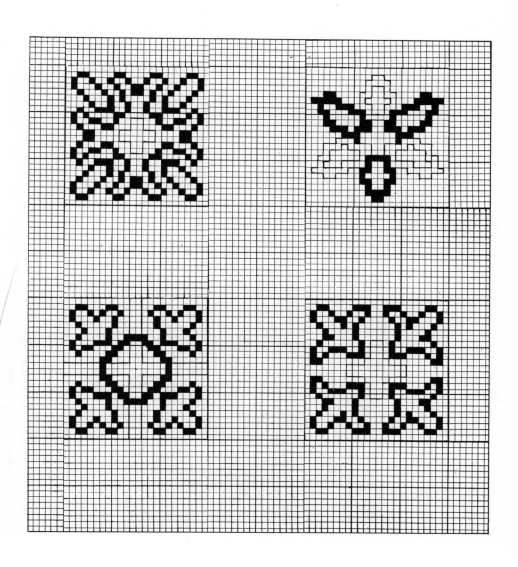

CHART 42

A Communion Kneeler
(Portuguese Design)

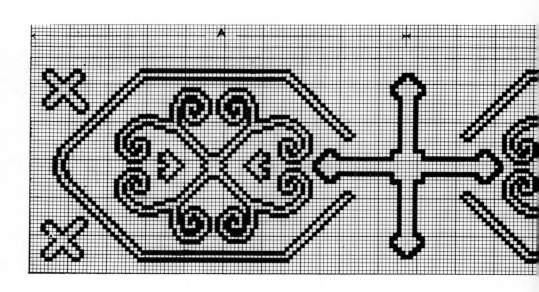

CANVAS   5s, open mesh
WIDTH   12″, 57 stitches (canvas = 58, 'lose' one stitch, see page 12)
LENGTH   It will be noticed that the chart is divided into three sections marked A, B
            and C. The length of the rug as charted is the total of the three sections, i.e.

$$
\begin{array}{ll}
\text{A} & 1'\ 7\frac{1}{2}'' \\
\text{B} & 1'\ 8'' \\
\text{C} & 1'\ 7\frac{1}{2}'' \\
\hline
& 4'\ 11'' \\
\hline
\end{array}
$$

Section B can be repeated as often as required to make the rug fit the Communion step, but it should be remembered that room must be allowed for the beginning and end of the rug (A and C). Approximate weight of wool required per yard run: 18 oz.

This design is based on the border of a Portuguese carpet.

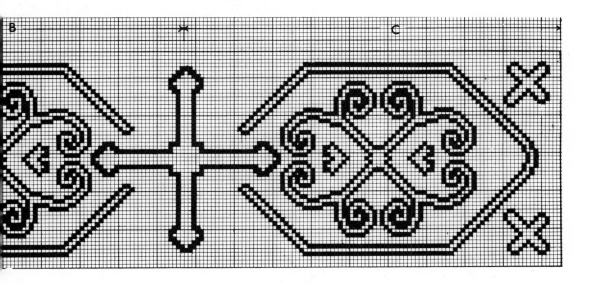

CHART 43

A Communion Kneeler
(Crown of Thorns)

CANVAS   10s, single mesh
WIDTH $11\frac{1}{2}''$
LENGTH   The Crown of Thorns and Cross can be repeated as often as required to fit
the length of the altar step, but it must be remembered that the rug must start
and finish with the Crown of Thorns and an end border.

For this single mesh canvas only one length of 2-ply wool in the needle is necessary.

It is suggested that the Crown of Thorns and its background should be worked in tent-stitch (over a single intersection of the single mesh canvas). The two lines enclosing the Crown of Thorns should be in back-stitch to mark where the tent-stitch ends and the background starts – long-legged cross-stitch in several shades of the selected main colour being suggested for this.

It should be noted that strongly contrasting colours are advisable for the border interlace, and for the Crown of Thorns which is shaded on the chart.

Approximate weight of wool required per yard run: 1¼ lbs.

Designed by Mr H. E. Turner, Marlborough.

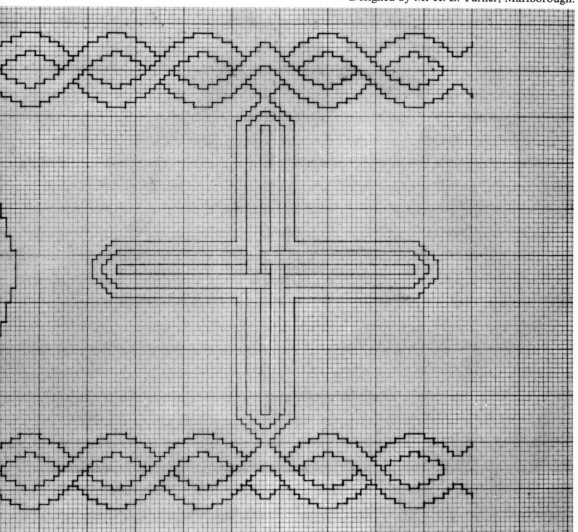

CHART 44

A Communion Kneeler
(Pelican Design)

CANVAS   10s, single mesh

WIDTH   10″

LENGTH   The Pelican and Cross can be repeated as often as required to fit the length of the altar step, but it must be remembered that the rug must start and finish with a Pelican and an end border.

For this single mesh canvas only one length of 2-ply wool in the needle is necessary.

It is suggested that the Pelican and its background should be worked in tent-stitch (over a single intersection of the single mesh canvas). The two lines enclosing the bird should be in back-stitch to mark where the tent-stitch ends and the background starts – long-legged cross-stitch in several shades of the selected main colour being suggested for this.

It should be noted that strongly contrasting colours are advisable for the border interlace.

Approximate weight of wool required per yard run: 1 lb.

Designed by Mr. H. E. Turner, Marlborough.

CHART 45   # The Dragon Rug

JUTE   4s (see Materials, Note 1, page 12)
WIDTH   36″, 144 stitches – with 21 stitch borders
LENGTH   57″, 228 stitches – with 21 stitch borders
Area of rug: $14\frac{1}{4}$ sq. ft.
Approximate weight of wool required: 7 lbs.

It is in answer to requests that the Dragon appears charted in this book as did his line-drawing at the beginning of *Needle-made Rugs*. His chart is the last because of his numerous faults, although he *has* been outlined which the original was not. His greatest fault is still obvious and once again I should like to remind all rug makers that the wear and tear on rugs is bound to be so great that they must be turned round frequently and therefore it is strongly advised that they should be designed to look well from whatever angle they are seen – and the Dragon does not conform in this respect.

Colours used

The original Dragon was the perfect Chinese blue and he pranced across a lovely self-coloured plate.

The main colour of the worked Dragon is a deep blue, the under-wings being a lighter shade of this, the claws dark yellow, the tongue scarlet and the spines black.

Shading has been used to indicate and clarify the colour changes.

As the Dragon makes such a large and definite splash of colour a quiet tone was obviously necessary for his background and a cream was chosen.

A border for this rug is optional but if one is worked it should be deep blue, 21 stitches wide all round. If the border is omitted the cream field should be extended to take its place.

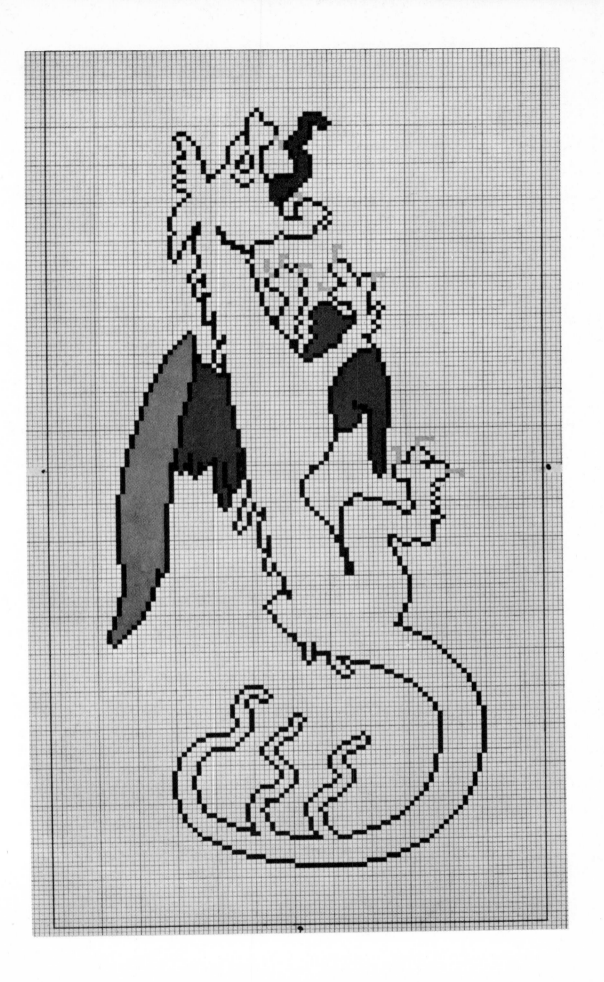

Ryijy (or Rya) Woven Rugs

A. A SHORT HISTORICAL NOTE

When browsing through books about Rya rugs it was somewhat daunting to find eight different versions of their name. The old Norse word Ry develops into the Finnish word Ryijy, but luckily the modern Swedish and Norwegian form is Rya – which is much the easier to spell.

Rya means a shaggy covering and the rugs are thought to have evolved from the rough and heavy wraps, made of impervious wool and having a long nap, used particularly by seal hunters and fishermen in the northern waters.

According to the great authority Professor U. T. Sirelius – whose book *The Ryijy Rugs of Finland* is fascinating and deserves endless study, the most important function of a Rya, from its inception as a real rug, was as a bed-covering.

Those who have seen the long-pile loom-woven Finnish rugs can well appreciate their comfort used thus – think of the winter of 1963. In addition anyone who had the good fortune (as did the writer) to visit the exhibition of Rya rugs at the Victoria and Albert Museum in 1958, and whose first impression on a dreary March day was the glorious splash of colour made by rug after rug, would realise that in a land where light was scanty during the winter months the comfort would be mental as well as physical.

By the fifteenth century the Ryas had evolved into knotted pile rugs and were used as coverings for seats, sledges, floors, and wall-hangings (on special occasions) although still chiefly for bed-covers.

An interesting and noteworthy point is that these rugs resembled the Oriental carpets in an important technical detail of their weaving. In both cases the tufts of yarn that covered the surface and formed the pile were (and still are) tied by the Ghiordes (Turkey) knot and it is thought possible that the art of carpet knotting and weaving may have been carried to the far north by the Crusaders. A difference in technique is that whereas Oriental carpets usually have only one or two threads of weft between the rows of knots, Scandinavian rugs have as a rule ten to twenty.

These early long-pile rugs had extremely simple designs and colouring – such as dark squares outlined in a light colour; black and white (or grey) diamonds (see Highway of the Sun Rug, Chart 3) – and were still soft and pliable as befitted their use as bed-coverings.

Later the designs became more elaborate and the pile shorter and thicker so that the decorative patterns becoming popular showed up clearly against the background. There are some fine examples of these to be seen at the Victoria and Albert Museum with characteristic designs and harmonious colouring.

The two types of rug developed hand in hand for many years, becoming classified as 'everyday' rugs (long pile) and 'decorative' rugs (short, dense pile), but even up to the beginning of the nineteenth century the majority of the Finnish rugs were of the long-pile type, generally of one colour only and of very simple geometrical design.

Many of the designs of the 'decorative' Ryas are said to date back to the Middle Ages and, having been used time and again by different workers, have naturally altered their forms and thus added to their general interest.

Throughout their history the rugs continued to be used in many ways. They formed an important item in every girl's dowry, and it was customary for the young couple to stand on their rug for the marriage ceremony, as illustrated by photographs in Sirelius's book.

Pages could be written about the fascinating features of these rugs, and this short introduction can give but a minute part of the story.

The 'modern' Rya rugs have developed since the 1930s, and have two distinctive features – they have reverted to the use of the long pile and their colouring is of an almost inconceivable brilliance.

Since *Needle-made Rugs* was published there has been a great wave of interest and enthusiasm for these 'tone' rugs and many people unable to weave began to wish that it was possible to make a rug with a needle and on a ready-made foundation that would produce much the same general effect as a 'real' woven Rya.

A few enthusiastic Women's Institute members have made a study of the possibilities of such an adaptation with great success and I am indebted to Mrs Droop for the following instructions.

B. RYA-TYPE RUGS – A NEEDLE-MADE ADAPTATION

Canvas – 4s open mesh.

Wool – 2-ply Axminster thrums in hanks.

Needles – a very large size is needed, 12 or 13, as four strands of wool are used simultaneously for the pile and three for the edging-stitch and flat-stitches between the rows of knots.

Quantity of wool required – 10 to 12 oz. per sq. ft.

Method of working – with Rya-type rugs the rows of pile are separated by rows of deep long-legged cross-stitch which are invisible in the finished rug. Incidentally, these rows of deep long-legged cross-stitch correspond to the numerous rows of weft between the knots in the Scandinavian rugs – see page 144, paragraph 6. The pile, worked in Surrey stitch or Turkey knot as preferred, should be 2 to 2½ inches in length.

1. After folding and stitching the cut edges of the canvas in the usual way, start the rug by working three rows of deep long-legged cross-stitch if for a 2 inch pile rug, and four rows if a 2½ inch pile is wanted.

2. In order to prevent the long pile from hanging over the selvedge edges it is advisable to work 3 stitches (covering 4 holes of the canvas) of ordinary long-legged cross-stitch at each selvedge edge of all the pile rows.

3. Work the first row of pile. When the row of loops has been finished and cut the pile should reach just to the end of the rug, including the edging-stitch.

4. Work two rows of deep long-legged cross-stitch if making a 2 inch pile rug and three rows for a 2½ inch pile.

5. Work the second row of pile, *not forgetting the 3 stitches in simple long-legged cross-stitch at each end of it*. This and subsequent rows of pile should, when trimmed, overlap the preceding row of pile by half its length.

6. The rug is finished by working one row of deep long-legged cross-stitch after the last row of pile.

Many people prefer to work all their deep long-legged cross-stitched background before starting their pile – during which the *unworked* length of the canvas will of course face towards the worker as for all smooth-faced rugs. The rug is then reversed and the pile rows worked with the full length of the canvas stretching *away* from the worker.

The above procedure is, of course, purely a matter of personal preference as with so much in rug making.

Designing for this type of rug lends itself to bold and abstract forms, and interesting patterns can be evolved during the actual working. A visit to Heal and Son Ltd, 196 Tottenham Court Road, London W.1, can be most rewarding when searching for ideas as they stock a large number of Rya rugs in their showrooms.

Those who have made short-pile rugs will remember how the simultaneous use of different near shades of a colour in the needle helps greatly in producing pleasing colour results, and with the 'modern' long-pile 'shaggy' rugs, carrying four lengths in the needle for the pile, it is obvious that this technique is particularly invaluable.

Subtle colour blending and the use of brilliant shades are vital to these rugs and add greatly to their beauty – in fact it is not too much to say that they stand or fall by their colouring.

Appendix 1   # Bibliography

1. *Hand Woven Carpets*, 2 vols, Kendrick and Tattersall.
   This is a stupendous work. One volume contains coloured plates and one the letterpress. It is a mine of fascinating information but is only to be found at large libraries.
2. *A History of British Carpets*, C. E. C. Tattersall (F. Lewis).
   A valuable book of reference and most interesting reading. It can be borrowed on request from branches of public libraries.
3. *The Rug (Le Tapis)*, Albert Achdijan (Editions Self, Paris).
   This book is printed in both English and French, is full of superb illustrations, many in excellent colours, and has reproductions of numerous small pictorial motifs which are a source of inspiration for designing.
4. *How to Identify Persian and Other Oriental Rugs*, G. J. Delabere May (G. Bell & Sons). 16*s*.
   A very useful and inexpensive book with numerous helpful illustrations.
5. *How to Know Oriental Carpets and Rugs*, Heinrich Jacoby (Allen & Unwin). 25*s*.
6. *A Practical Book of Oriental Rugs*, G. Griffin Lewis (Lippincott, U.S.A.).
   Can be borrowed from public libraries.
7. *Notes on Carpet Knotting and Weaving*, C. E. C. Tattersall (Victoria and Albert Museum). 2*s*. 6*d*.
   A 'must' for all rug makers. It is invaluable in many ways and amazingly inexpensive.
8. *Dictionary of Embroidery Stitches*, Mary Thomas (Hodder & Stoughton). 15*s*.
   A comprehensive work on embroidery stitches generally, including many that are suitable for rug making.
9. *Ecclesiastical Embroidery*, Beryl Dean (Batsford). £2 10*s*.
   A book that should be consulted by those making rugs and carpets for churches – many valuable references to the use of symbolism.
10. *Needle-made Rugs*, Sibyl I. Mathews (Mills & Boon). 40*s*. (3rd edn).
    Detailed instructions on stitches, choice of wools and canvas, and other points of technique. Illustrated with photographs, diagrams and charts.
11. *Oriental Rugs*, Hermann Haack, tr. G. and C. Wingfield Digby (Faber & Faber). 35*s*.
12. Portfolios 2, 6, 10 Lts. Forlag, Stockholm. 15*s*. 6*d*. each.
    Good designs for adaptations. The Tiranti Bookshop, 72 Charlotte Street, London W.1, and Miss K. R. Drummond, 30 Hart Grove, Ealing Common, London W.5, stock these portfolios.
13. Many of the D.M.C. publications are useful when looking for ideas for designs.

Appendix 2   Suppliers of Materials

The firms listed are those of which I have had personal experience. There are, no doubt, many others equally reliable and rug-making materials are advertised in many magazines, e.g. *Home and Country* (the Women's Institute magazine) and *Embroidery* (the Journal of the Embroiderers' Guild). Readers in the U.S.A. will find guidance in the 'yellow pages' of their local directories.

Prices are not quoted as they vary from time to time and place to place but, surprisingly, rug materials have not risen appreciably during the last few years. The lists which follow show the main suppliers at the time of writing (March 1967), but it should be realised that in these difficult times changes in the lines which a supplier stocks are inevitable, therefore rug makers are strongly advised to write to several firms for patterns and prices before embarking upon a rug.

WOOL

1. 6-ply thick wool

Jackson's Rug-Craft Centre, Croft Mill, Hebden Bridge, Nr. Halifax, Yorks.
Loomcraft, Southside, Headcorn Road, Sutton Valence, Kent.
The Needlewoman Shop, 146–8 Regent Street, London W.1.
The Royal Wilton Carpet Factory, Wilton, Nr. Salisbury, Wilts.
Spinning Jenny, Bradley, Keighley, Yorks.
The Winwood Textile Co., Lisle Avenue, Kidderminster, Worcs.

2. 2-ply carpet thrums

As above, also
Reginald Parker and Co. Ltd, 46 George Street, Ayr.

The prices of thrums vary according to the lengths of wool in the bundles. 2-ply wool in separate colours, either in whole or broken hanks, can generally be supplied by the above firms although it is naturally more expensive than the mixed colours.

3. Fine wool

A. *Brussels thrums or worsted*

Jackson's Rug-Craft Centre.
Loomcraft.
Spinning Jenny.
The Royal Wilton Carpet Factory.
The Winwood Textile Co.

B. *Crewel wool*
    Loomcraft.
    Mace and Nairn, Crane Street, Salisbury, Wilts.
    The Needlewoman Shop.
    Spinning Jenny.
   Nearly all needlework shops stock a complete range of reliable crewel wools, including the well-known Appleton's and Penelope's.

CANVAS

1. Double mesh

A. *3s, 4s and 5s*
    Jackson's Rug-Craft Centre.
    Mace and Nairn.
    The Needlewoman Shop.
    Reginald Parker.
    The Royal Wilton Carpet Factory.
    The Winwood Textile Co.

B. *7s and above*
    Harrods, Knightsbridge (linen).
    Loomcraft (except 7s).
    Mace and Nairn (linen).
    The Needlewoman Shop.
    Spinning Jenny.

2. Single mesh

A. *8s jute*
    Jackson's Rug-Craft Centre.
    Loomcraft.
    Mace and Nairn.
    The Needlewoman Shop.
    The Royal Wilton Carpet Factory.
    Spinning Jenny.

B. *Single mesh 'open' canvas 10 holes to the inch*
    Dryads Ltd, 93 Great Russell Street, London W.C.1 (cotton).
    The Royal Wilton Carpet Factory (cotton).
    Loomcraft (linen).
    Mace and Nairn (linen).
    The Winwood Textile Co.

NEEDLES

These should be blunt-pointed and large enough for the wool used to slip easily through the eye. Sizes 13 to 16 are recommended for use with coarse canvas, 18 to 22 for 7s and upwards.
    Dryads.
    Jackson's Rug-Craft Centre.
    Loomcraft.
    Mace and Nairn.
    The Needlewoman Shop.
    Spinning Jenny.
    The Royal Wilton Carpet Factory.

U.S.A.

WHOLESALE SUPPLIERS
(write them for names of stores nearest you)

Boye Needle Co., 916 S. Arcade Ave., Freeport, Ill. 61032. *Needles.*

Emile Bernat & Sons Co., Depot and Mendon Sts., Uxbridge, Mass. 01569. *Canvas, needles.*

Paternayan Bros., Inc., 312 E. 95th St., New York, N.Y. 10028. *Canvas, wools, needles.*

Joan Toggitt Ltd., 1170 Broadway, Suite 406, New York, N.Y. 10001. *Canvas, wools, needles.*

SUPPLIERS OF MATERIALS
(all will fill mail orders)

Herrschners, Inc., Hoover Rd., Stevens Point, Wisc. 54481. *Wools, needles.*

Lee Wards, Elgin, Ill. 60120. *Canvas, wools, needles.*

The Mannings-Creative Crafts, R.D. #2, E. Berlin, Pa., 17316. *Canvas, wools, needles.*

Merribee Needle Art Co., 2904 W. Lancaster St., Ft. Worth, Texas 76107. *Canvas, wools.*

Needlecraft House, W. Townsend, Mass. 01474. *Canvas, wools, needles.*

Needlecraft Shop, 13561 Ventura Blvd., Sherman Oaks, Calif. 91403. *Canvas, wools, needles.*

Norden Products, P.O. Box 1, Glenview, Ill. 60025. *Canvas, wools, needles.*

Scandinavian Art Handicraft, 7696 Camargo Rd., Madeira, Cincinnati, Ohio 45243. *Canvas, wools, needles.*

Joan Toggitt Ltd., 1170 Broadway, Suite 406, New York, N.Y. 10001. *Canvas, wools, needles.*

Dover Books on Art

MASTERPIECES OF FURNITURE, Verna Cook Salomonsky. Photographs and measured drawings of some of the finest examples of Colonial American, 17th century English, Windsor, Sheraton, Hepplewhite, Chippendale, Louis XIV, Queen Anne, and various other furniture styles. The textual matter includes information on traditions, characteristics, background, etc. of various pieces. 101 plates. Bibliography. 224pp. 7⅞ x 10¾.
21381-1 Paperbound $4.00

PRIMITIVE ART, Franz Boas. In this exhaustive volume, a great American anthropologist analyzes all the fundamental traits of primitive art, covering the formal element in art, representative art, symbolism, style, literature, music, and the dance. Illustrations of Indian embroidery, paleolithic paintings, woven blankets, wing and tail designs, totem poles, cutlery, earthenware, baskets and many other primitive objects and motifs. Over 900 illustrations. 376pp. 5⅜ x 8.   20025-6 Paperbound $3.50

AN INTRODUCTION TO A HISTORY OF WOODCUT, A. M. Hind. Nearly all of this authoritative 2-volume set is devoted to the 15th century—the period during which the woodcut came of age as an important art form. It is the most complete compendium of information on this period, the artists who contributed to it, and their technical and artistic accomplishments. Profusely illustrated with cuts by 15th century masters, and later works for comparative purposes. 484 illustrations. 5 indexes. Total of xi + 838pp. 5⅜ x 8½. Two-vols. 20952-0, 20953-0 Paperbound $8.50

A HISTORY OF ENGRAVING AND ETCHING, A. M. Hind. Beginning with the anonymous masters of 15th century engraving, this highly regarded and thorough survey carries you through Italy, Holland, and Germany to the great engravers and beginnings of etching in the 16th century, through the portrait engravers, master etchers, practicioners of mezzotint, crayon manner and stipple, aquatint, color prints, to modern etching in the period just prior to World War I. Beautifully illustrated —sharp clear prints on heavy opaque paper. Author's preface. 3 appendixes. 111 illustrations. xviii + 487 pp. 5⅜ x 8½.
20954-7 Paperbound $5.00

ART STUDENTS' ANATOMY, E. J. Farris. Teaching anatomy by using chiefly living objects for illustration, this study has enjoyed long popularity and success in art courses and home-study programs. All the basic elements of the human anatomy are illustrated in minute detail, diagrammed and pictured as they pass through common movements and actions. 158 drawings, photographs, and roentgenograms. Glossary of anatomical terms. x + 159pp. 5⅝ x 8⅜.   20744-7 Paperbound $2.00

COLONIAL LIGHTING, A. H. Hayward. The only book to cover the fascinating story of lamps and other lighting devices in America. Beginning with rush light holders used by the early settlers, it ranges through the elaborate chandeliers of the Federal period, illustrating 647 lamps. Of great value to antique collectors, designers, and historians of arts and crafts. Revised and enlarged by James R. Marsh. xxxi + 198pp. 5⅝ x 8¼.
20975-X Paperbound $2.50

200 DECORATIVE TITLE-PAGES, edited by A. Nesbitt. Fascinating and informative from a historical point of view, this beautiful collection of decorated titles will be a great inspiration to students of design, commercial artists, advertising designers, etc. A complete survey of the genre from the first known decorated title to work in the first decades of this century. Bibliography and sources of the plates. 222pp. 8⅜ x 11¼.

21264-5 Paperbound $3.50

ON THE LAWS OF JAPANESE PAINTING, H. P. Bowie. This classic work on the philosophy and technique of Japanese art is based on the author's first-hand experiences studying art in Japan. Every aspect of Japanese painting is described: the use of the brush and other materials; laws governing conception and execution; subjects for Japanese paintings, etc. The best possible substitute for a series of lessons from a great Oriental master. Index. xv + 117pp. + 66 plates. 6⅛ x 9¼.

20030-2 Paperbound $4.00

A HANDBOOK OF ANATOMY FOR ART STUDENTS, Arthur Thomson. This long-popular text teaches any student, regardless of level of technical competence, all the subtleties of human anatomy. Clear photographs, numerous line sketches and diagrams of bones, joints, etc. Use it as a text for home study, as a supplement to life class work, or as a lifelong sourcebook and reference volume. Author's prefaces. 67 plates, containing 40 line drawings, 86 photographs—mostly full page. 211 figures. Appendix. Index. xx + 459pp. 5⅜ x 8⅜. 21163-0 Paperbound $5.00

WHITTLING AND WOODCARVING, E. J. Tangerman. With this book, a beginner who is moderately handy can whittle or carve scores of useful objects, toys for children, gifts, or simply pass hours creatively and enjoyably. "Easy as well as instructive reading," N. Y. Herald Tribune Books. 464 illustrations, with appendix and index. x + 293pp. 5½ x 8⅛.

20965-2 Paperbound $2.50

ONE HUNDRED AND ONE PATCHWORK PATTERNS, Ruby Short McKim. Whether you have made a hundred quilts or none at all, you will find this the single most useful book on quiltmaking. There are 101 full patterns (all exact size) with full instructions for cutting and sewing. In addition there is some really choice folklore about the origin of the ingenious pattern names: "Monkey Wrench," "Road to California," "Drunkard's Path," "Crossed Canoes," to name a few. Over 500 illustrations. 124 pp. 7⅞ x 10¾. 20773-0 Paperbound $2.50

ART AND GEOMETRY, W. M. Ivins, Jr. Challenges the idea that the foundations of modern thought were laid in ancient Greece. Pitting Greek tactile-muscular intuitions of space against modern visual intuitions, the author, for 30 years curator of prints, Metropolitan Museum of Art, analyzes the differences between ancient and Renaissance painting and sculpture and tells of the first fruitful investigations of perspective. x + 113pp. 5⅜ x 8⅜. 20941-5 Paperbound $2.00

THE FOUR BOOKS OF ARCHITECTURE, Andrea Palladio. A compendium of the art of Andrea Palladio, one of the most celebrated architects of the Renaissance, including 250 magnificently-engraved plates showing edifices either of Palladio's design or reconstructed (in these drawings) by him from classical ruins and contemporary accounts. 257 plates. xxiv + 119pp. 9½ x 12¾. 21308-0 Clothbound $12.50

150 MASTERPIECES OF DRAWING, A. Toney. Selected by a gifted artist and teacher, these are some of the finest drawings produced by Western artists from the early 15th to the end of the 18th centuries. Excellent reproductions of drawings by Rembrandt, Bruegel, Raphael, Watteau, and other familiar masters, as well as works by lesser known but brilliant artists. 150 plates. xviii + 150pp. 5⅜ x 11¼. 21032-4 Paperbound $3.50

MORE DRAWINGS BY HEINRICH KLEY. Another collection of the graphic, vivid sketches of Heinrich Kley, one of the most diabolically talented cartoonists of our century. The sketches take in every aspect of human life: nothing is too sacred for him to ridicule, no one too eminent for him to satirize. 158 drawings you will not easily forget. iv + 104pp. 7⅜ x 10¾. 20041-8 Paperbound $2.00

THE TRIUMPH OF MAXIMILIAN I, 137 Woodcuts by Hans Burgkmair and Others. This is one of the world's great art monuments, a series of magnificent woodcuts executed by the most important artists in the German realms as part of an elaborate plan by Maximilian I, ruler of the Holy Roman Empire, to commemorate his own name, dynasty, and achievements. 137 plates. New translation of descriptive text, notes, and bibliography prepared by Stanley Appelbaum. Special section of 10pp. containing a reduced version of the entire Triumph. x + 169pp. 11⅛ x 9¼. 21207-6 Paperbound $3.50

PAINTING IN ISLAM, Sir Thomas W. Arnold. This scholarly study puts Islamic painting in its social and religious context and examines its relation to Islamic civilization in general. 65 full-page plates illustrate the text and give outstanding examples of Islamic art. 4 appendices. Index of mss. referred to. General Index. xxiv + 159pp. 6⅝ x 9¼. 21310-2 Paperbound $3.00

THE MATERIALS AND TECHNIQUES OF MEDIEVAL PAINTING, D. V. Thompson. An invaluable study of carriers and grounds, binding media, pigments, metals used in painting, al fresco and al secco techniques, burnishing, etc. used by the medieval masters. Preface by Bernard Berenson. 239pp. 5⅜ x 8. 20327-1 Paperbound $3.00

THE HISTORY AND TECHNIQUE OF LETTERING, A. Nesbitt. A thorough history of lettering from the ancient Egyptians to the present, and a 65-page course in lettering for artists. Every major development in lettering history is illustrated by a complete aphabet. Fully analyzes such masters as Caslon, Koch, Garamont, Jenson, and many more. 89 alphabets, 165 other specimens. 317pp. 7½ x 10½. 20427-8 Paperbound $4.00

AFRICAN SCULPTURE, Ladislas Segy. 163 full-page plates illustrating masks, fertility figures, ceremonial objects, etc., of 50 West and Central African tribes—95% never before illustrated. 34-page introduction to African sculpture. "Mr. Segy is one of its top authorities," NEW YORKER. 164 full-page photographic plates. Introduction. Bibliography. 244pp. 6⅛ x 9¼.

20396-4 Paperbound $3.00

CALLIGRAPHY, J. G. Schwandner. First reprinting in 200 years of this legendary book of beautiful handwriting. Over 300 ornamental initials, 12 complete calligraphic alphabets, over 150 ornate frames and panels, 75 calligraphic pictures of cherubs, stags, lions, etc., thousands of flourishes, scrolls, etc., by the greatest 18th-century masters. All material can be copied or adapted without permission. Historical introduction. 158 full-page plates. 368pp. 9 x 13.   20475-8   Clothbound $12.50

PRINTED EPHEMERA, edited and collected by John Lewis. This book contains centuries of design, typographical and pictorial motives in proven, effective commercial layouts. Hundreds of the most striking examples of labels, tickets, posters, wrappers, programs, menus, and other items have been collected in this handsome and useful volume, along with information on the dimensions and colors of the original, printing processes used, stylistic notes on typography and design, etc. Study this book and see how the best commercial artists of the past and present have solved their particular problems. Most of the material is copyright free. 713 illustrations, many in color. Illustrated index of type faces included. Glossary of technical terms. Indexes. 288pp. 9¼ x 12.   22284-5, 22285-3   Clothbound $15.00

DESIGN FOR ARTISTS AND CRAFTSMEN, Louis Wolchonok. Recommended for either individual or classroom use, this book helps you to create original designs from things about you, from geometric patterns, from plants, animals, birds, humans, landscapes, manmade objects. "A great contribution," N. Y. Society of Craftsmen. 113 exercises with hints and diagrams. More than 1280 illustrations. xv + 207pp. 7⅞ x 10¾.

20274-7   Paperbound $3.50

HANDBOOK OF ORNAMENT, F. S. Meyer. One of the largest collections of copyright-free traditional art: over 3300 line cuts of Greek, Roman, Medieval, Renaissance, Baroque, 18th and 19th century art motifs (tracery, geometric elements, flower and animal motifs, etc.) and decorated objects (chairs, thrones, weapons, vases, jewelry, armor, etc.). Full text. 300 plates. 3300 illustrations. 562pp. 5⅜ x 8.   20302-6   Paperbound $4.50

THREE CLASSICS OF ITALIAN CALLIGRAPHY, Oscar Ogg, ed. Exact reproductions of three famous Renaissance calligraphic works: Arrighi's OPERINA and IL MODO, Tagliente's LO PRESENTE LIBRO, and Palatino's LIBRO NUOVO. More than 200 complete alphabets, thousands of lettered specimens, in Papal Chancery and other beautiful, ornate handwriting. Introduction. 245 plates. 282pp. 6⅛ x 9¼.   20212-7   Paperbound $4.00

VASARI ON TECHNIQUE, G. Vasari. Pupil of Michelangelo, outstanding biographer of Renaissance artists reveals technical methods of his day. Marble, bronze, fresco painting, mosaics, engraving, stained glass, rustic ware, etc. Only English translation, extensively annotated by G. Baldwin Brown. 18 plates. 342pp. 5⅜ x 8.   20717-X Paperbound $3.50

FOOT-HIGH LETTERS: A GUIDE TO LETTERING, M. Price. 28 15½ x 22½″ plates, give classic Roman alphabet, one foot high per letter, plus 9 other 2″ high letter forms for each letter. 16 page syllabus. Ideal for lettering classes, home study. 28 plates in box.   20238-9 $8.50

A HANDBOOK OF WEAVES, G. H. Oelsner. Most complete book of weaves, fully explained, differentiated, illustrated. Plain weaves, irregular, double-stitched, filling satins; derivative, basket, rib weaves; steep, broken, herringbone, twills, lace, tricot, many others. Translated, revised by S. S. Dale; supplement on analysis of weaves. Bible for all handweavers. 1875 illustrations. 410pp. 6⅛ x 9¼.   20209-7 Clothbound $7.50

JAPANESE HOMES AND THEIR SURROUNDINGS, E. S. Morse. Classic describes, analyses, illustrates all aspects of traditional Japanese home, from plan and structure to appointments, furniture, etc. Published in 1886, before Japanese architecture was contaminated by Western, this is strikingly modern in beautiful, functional approach to living. Indispensable to every architect, interior decorator, designer. 307 illustrations. Glossary. 410pp. 5⅝ x 8⅜.   20746-3 Paperbound $3.50

THE DRAWINGS OF HEINRICH KLEY. Uncut publication of long-sought-after sketchbooks of satiric, ironic iconoclast. Remarkable fantasy, weird symbolism, brilliant technique make Kley a shocking experience to layman, endless source of ideas, techniques for artist. 200 drawings, original size, captions translated. Introduction. 136pp. 6 x 9.   20024-8 Paperbound $3.00

COSTUMES OF THE ANCIENTS, Thomas Hope. Beautiful, clear, sharp line drawings of Greek and Roman figures in full costume, by noted artist and antiquary of early 19th century. Dress, armor, divinities, masks, etc. Invaluable sourcebook for costumers, designers, first-rate picture file for illustrators, commercial artists. Introductory text by Hope. 300 plates. 6 x 9.   20021-3 Paperbound $3.95

EPOCHS OF CHINESE AND JAPANESE ART, E. Fenollosa. Classic study of pre-20th century Oriental art, revealing, as does no other book, the important interrelationships between the art of China and Japan and their history and sociology. Illustrations include ancient bronzes, Buddhist paintings by Kobo Daishi, scroll paintings by Toba Sojo, prints by Nobusane, screens by Korin, woodcuts by Hokusai, Koryusai, Utamaro, Hiroshige and scores of other pieces by Chinese and Japanese masters. Biographical preface. Notes. Index. 242 illustrations. Total of lii + 439pp. plus 174 plates. 5⅝ x 8¼.

20364-6, 20265-4 Two-volume set, Paperbound $8.00

Dover Books on Art

LANDSCAPE GARDENING IN JAPAN, Josiah Conder. A detailed picture of Japanese gardening techniques and ideas, the artistic principles incorporated in the Japanese garden, and the religious and ethical concepts at the heart of those principles. Preface. 92 illustrations, plus all 40 full-page plates from the Supplement. Index. xv + 299pp. 8⅜ x 11¼.

21216-5   Paperbound .$4.50

DESIGN AND FIGURE CARVING, E. J. Tangerman. "Anyone who can peel a potato can carve," states the author, and in this unusual book he shows you how, covering every stage in detail from very simple exercises working up to museum-quality pieces. Terrific aid for hobbyists, arts and crafts counselors, teachers, those who wish to make reproductions for the commercial market. Appendix: How to Enlarge a Design. Brief bibliography. Index. 1298 figures. x + 289pp. 5⅜ x 8½.

21209-2   Paperbound $3.00

THE STANDARD BOOK OF QUILT MAKING AND COLLECTING, M. Ickis. Even if you are a beginner, you will soon find yourself quilting like an expert, by following these clearly drawn patterns, photographs, and step-by-step instructions. Learn how to plan the quilt, to select the pattern to harmonize with the design and color of the room, to choose materials. Over 40 full-size patterns. Index. 483 illustrations. One color plate. xi + 276pp. 6¾ x 9½.   20582-7   Paperbound $3.50

LOST EXAMPLES OF COLONIAL ARCHITECTURE, J. M. Howells. This book offers a unique guided tour through America's architectural past, all of which is either no longer in existence or so changed that its original beauty has been destroyed. More than 275 clear photos of old churches, dwelling houses, public buildings, business structures, etc. 245 plates, containing 281 photos and 9 drawings, floorplans, etc. New Index. xvii + 248pp. 7⅞ x 10¾.   21143-6   Paperbound $3.50

A HISTORY OF COSTUME, Carl Köhler. The most reliable and authentic account of the development of dress from ancient times through the 19th century. Based on actual pieces of clothing that have survived, using paintings, statues and other reproductions only where originals no longer exist. Hundreds of illustrations, including detailed patterns for many articles. Highly useful for theatre and movie directors, fashion designers, illustrators, teachers. Edited and augmented by Emma von Sichart. Translated by Alexander K. Dallas. 594 illustrations. 464pp. 5⅛ x 7⅛.

21030-8   Paperbound $4.50

Dover publishes books on commercial art, art history, crafts, design, art classics; also books on music, literature, science, mathematics, puzzles and entertainments, chess, engineering, biology, philosophy, psychology, languages, history, and other fields. For free circulars write to Dept. DA, Dover Publications, Inc., 180 Varick St., New York, N.Y. 10014.